THE ELEMENTS OF BUDDHISM

John Snelling, world-renowned Buddhist scholar, died in 1991. He was born in Wales in 1943 and brought up there, as well as in London and Canterbury. After graduating with honours degrees in both English and Philosophy, he lectured at Maidstone College of Art for a number of years before leaving to travel in the East, where his interest in Oriental religion and philosophy really began. From 1980 until 1984 he was General Secretary of the Buddhist Society, and from 1980 to 1987 he was the Editor of the Society's quarterly journal, *The Middle Way*, which is believed to be the most widely circulated Buddhist periodical in the West, perhaps in the world. John Snelling has written numerous books and articles, as well as stories, plays and features for radio and television.

The *Elements Of* is a series designed to present high quality introductions to a broad range of essential subjects.

The books are commissioned specifically from experts in their fields. They provide readable and often unique views of the various topics covered, and are therefore of interest both to those who have some knowledge of the subject, as well as those who are approaching it for the first time.

Many of these concise yet comprehensive books have practical suggestions and exercises which allow personal experiences as well as theoretical understanding, and offer a valuable source of information on many important themes.

In the same series

The Aborigine Tradition	Human Potential
Alchemy	Islam
The Arthurian Tradition	Judaism
Astrology	Meditation
The Bahá'í Faith	Mysticism
Celtic Christianity	Native American Traditions
The Celtic Tradition	Natural Magic
The Chakras	Pendulum Dowsing
Christian Symbolism	Prophecy
Creation Myth	Psychosynthesis
Dreamwork	The Qabalah
The Druid Tradition	The Runes
Earth Mysteries	Shamanism
The Egyptian Wisdom	Sufism
Feng Shui	Tai Chi
Gnosticism	Taoism
The Goddess	The Tarot
The Grail Tradition	Visualisation
Herbalism	Zen

THE ELEMENTS OF

BUDDHISM

John Snelling

ELEMENT

Shaftesbury, Dorset ● Rockport, Massachusetts
Brisbane, Queensland

© John Snelling 1990

First published in Great Britain in 1990 by
Element Books Limited
Shaftesbury, Dorset

Reprinted 1991
Reprinted 1992
Reprinted 1993
Reprinted March and September 1994

Published in the USA in 1991 by
Element Inc.
42 Broadway, Rockport, MA 01966

Published in Australia in 1992 by
Element Books Limited for
Jacaranda Wiley Limited
33 Park Road, Milton, Brisbane, 4064

Cover design by Max Fairbrother
Maps by Christopher Shaw
Typeset by Selectmove Ltd, London
Printed and bound in Great Britain by
Biddles Ltd., Guildford & King's Lynn

British Library Cataloguing in Publication Data
Snelling, John 1943-1991
The elements of Buddhism.
1. Buddhism
I. Title
294.3

Library of Congress Cataloging–in–Publication Data
Snelling, John, 1943-1991
The elements of Buddhism
Includes bibliographical references and index
1. Buddhism
I. Title   II. Series
294.3 dc20

ISBN 1–85230–172–4

CONTENTS

For my daughter
SARAH SNELLING
with much love.

All the Buddha's teachings have just this single object –
To carry us beyond the stage of thought.

Ch'an Master Huang-po

PREFACE

Most surveys of Buddhism are written from the point of view of a particular school or tradition. Here, however, we attempt to chart a concise and unbiased overview of the whole panorama of Buddhist doctrine, practice and history. In the course of this ecumenical endeavour, we trace the ways in which particular teachings and practices have changed and developed over the millennia in different contexts. For Buddhist doctrines and practices are not apart from life; they are dynamic and kinetic, like all vital things.

Buddhism has two canonical languages, Pali and Sanskrit. To avoid confusion, I have used Sanskrit terms, kept accents to the minimum and dropped diacritical marks, which are unfamiliar to non-academic Westerners. I have also, in some cases, amended the spelling of words, rendering them in simple phonetic forms. No Glossary is included, the meanings of technical terms being explained internally in the text. Major and minor references are indicated in the Notes and References section.

I should like to thank the following for their kind help: Stephen Batchelor, Martine Batchelor, Ajahn Anando, Richard Hunn, Rob Preece, Roger Wheeler and Diana St. Ruth.

This caveat is finally offered to the reader. As Buddhism ultimately deals with the ineffable, anything that is said must always be regarded as strictly provisional. Spirit, which is elusive and anarchic, cannot really be captured or fixed. Like the wind, it comes and goes according to its own mysterious ways. Therefore treat everything in this book lightly. If it is useful to you in helping you find your own way, use it. If not, discard it. And never treat it as a substitute for the wisdom that arises at clear moments in your own inner core.

Sharpham, Devon, 1990

INTRODUCTION

Many years ago, when I was trekking through the Nepalese Himalaya en route for Mount Everest, I found myself one evening in a small Sherpa village. With nothing else to do, I went over to look at the local Buddhist temple, a venerable building in the Tibetan style that was apparently little used.

Inside all was dark but gradually my eyes became accustomed to the gloom. Then I could see a phantasmagoria of benign and wrathful deities dancing on the walls, their once brilliant colours coated with brown soot from the butter-lamps that had flickeringly illuminated the temple for centuries.

My attention was drawn by the glint of gold and copper. I walked cautiously across the room, picking my way between vermilion pillars and among ancient moth-eaten cushions, to a small shrine. There I found a jumble of ancient votive objects. I began to examine them . . .

Almost at once I was seized by a disquieting sense of being watched. I checked behind . . . Nothing . . . To either side . . . Nothing . . . When I looked up, however, a sharp pang of surprise went through me. A huge gilded Buddha was sitting, partially concealed, in a chimney-like shaft behind the main shrine, and he was staring down at me, a faint smile playing across those colossal lips, as though he was amused at my initial unawareness of his presence. It was so obviously a benign and good-humoured smile that I could only return it. It also seemed to be telling me something.

That incident must have happened all of eighteen years ago now. Though slight enough in itself, it forged an important connection. I have been deeply involved in Buddhism ever since – delving into

1

the great mystery of the Buddha's smile. This small book is a brief summary of what I have discovered.

Buddhism is a jewel from the treasure-house of Indian spirituality. It emerged about 2,500 years ago in the central plain of the River Ganges, just south of the Himalayas, which, in all their snowy grandeur, stand as soaring symbols of the spiritual aspirations of the human race. Over the centuries Buddhism has been transmitted to many other countries and in the process has absorbed much of local tradition and undergone exciting new phases of development, but its Indian elements have always remained central and fundamental.

The established form of religion prevalent in India 2,500 years ago was Brahminism. Here a privileged caste of priests mediated between the ordinary people and the gods by controlling specialised religious rites. This tradition – the Vedas were its holy writings – was largely the creation of the dynamic Aryan people who invaded India during the first millennium BCE, though it also drew upon indigenous elements.

Buddhism, on the other hand, emerged from an alternative and rather different religious stream, the origins of which predate the Aryan invasions. This is an ancient yogic tradition, originally without professional priesthood or formal organisation, which places primary emphasis on direct personal penetration of the ultimate mysteries of life.

Since time immemorial pious Indians have venerated those spiritual seekers who have gone off alone into the tangled mountains and untamed jungles to discover truth for themselves. A sophisticated spiritual technology evolved to meet their needs: special yogas and meditation practices that, if correctly and diligently applied, might open the eye of wisdom and reveal Ultimate Reality, which is always sought within – in the human heart. Archaeologists digging in the ruins of the cities of the Indus Valley, Mohenjo Daro and Harappa, which had crumbled into the dust long before the first Aryan crossed the Indus, found very ancient images of such yogis sitting cross-legged in the lotus posture.

Although originally unsystematic and anarchic, around 600 BCE some groups of yogis, who had gathered around particular teachers or shramana, began to feel the need to present a more coherent and organised face to the world. At the time an economic revolution was under way in the middle Ganges region. New prosperity had created bustling commercial towns and cities populated by classes of *nouveaux riches* who had both the leisure and inclination for philosophical and religious inquiry. The Buddha was just such a teacher, and it was proverbially from among the 'young men of good

The Wheel of Life

family' that he drew many of his first disciples. Of the other shramana groups originally active, the only other one that survives today is the Nigrantha or Jains: the followers of Mahavira.

In order to understand Buddhism, it is useful to have a clear idea of the cosmology in which its teachings evolved.

The early Buddhists accepted the view of the Universe generally held in India at the time, though they modified it somewhat. Fundamental is the idea that time is not linear but circular. Consequently, the Universe is not created out of nothing at a particular point, nor will it be completely destroyed at another; it has always existed and will always exist. In the meantime, however, it goes through endless cycles of creation and destruction, creation and destruction – over and over and over . . .

Any being that is born into this cyclic Universe is the result of something that has gone before; or, in Buddhist parlance, he, she or it is the fruit (vipaka) of a preceding cause or willed action (karma). This is the doctrine of creation by causes. In turn, when any being dies, he, she or it creates the causes for the birth of a new being. All of us, then, are not living separate, individual lives, but are links in an endless circular or spiralling chain that reaches back into the beginningless past and forward into the endless future. This is not precisely reincarnation, for it is not exactly the same being that commutes from body to body down through the procession of the ages. The vital connection between one life and its successor is more subtle than that. We can say that it is not the same being that moves along the chain, but not a different being either; or we can say it is both the same and a different being. The appropriate word to describe this process is 'rebirth'.

Now, the main problem bearing on any human being is that their next rebirth may not be in the human realm. In fact the odds are very heavily loaded against it. Classical Buddhism specifies five or six realms or 'destinations' in which it is possible for rebirth to take place:

1. the heavens (the realms of the devas or gods, plus some rarefied regions above them);
2. the realm of the asuras or titans, who, like their Greek counterparts, are the bellicose old gods;
3. the realm of humans;
4. of animals;
5. of preta or hungry ghosts; and

6. the hell realms, which in Buddhist writings are numerous and exceedingly nasty.[1] So the whole system is fraught, for only two destinations are pleasant; the rest are painful, most direly so.

Rebirth, therefore, is a process of endless, uncontrollable circulation through a variety of mostly painful situations. By this token, merely to be born is distinctly bad news!

What keeps Samsara, the wheel of cyclic existence (see page 3), in perpetual spin? Basically it is trishna – thirst/craving/desire – not merely in its gross forms of wanting desirables and not wanting undesirables, but in extremely subtle ones, such as the basic undercurrent wish to exist. Trishna arises on a basis of delusion/ignorance (avidya), which is not just a blissful not-knowing but a kind of wilful blindness that refuses to face the true reality of a Universe of constant change and suffering. Anger/hatred, dvesha in Sanskrit, joins trishna and avidya to form an unholy Gang of Three, often called the Three Fires or Poisons.

This points directly to the main objective of the Buddhist project. This is not, as in the Western religions, to define and worship a Creator God. Though he did not much like speaking about them, the Buddha never denied the existence of gods; but in his cosmology even the highest of them is still a victim of the system because his tenure of his godly privileges, though running to many aeons, will still some day come to an end. Inevitably, then, he too must undergo a very real fall from grace and be recirculated through the system.

Nor is the highest aim of Buddhism to ensure access to some kind of eternal heaven after death. As we have seen, heavens were certainly thought to exist: the heavens of the gods and, above them, hierarchies of increasingly rarefied 'bliss states' (dhyanas), which might be reached by yogic disciplines. The Jains, through exceedingly rigorous ascetic practice and the accumulation of the necessary merit, sought access to the highest of these states. But that too was strictly temporary.

No, what the Buddha sought was an Exit – final and total release from cyclic existence; escape from Samsara once and for all; never again to be subject to rebirth and its attendant miseries. This is Liberation, Moksha, Enlightenment, Nirvana. . .

Every great religion is founded by what we might call a spiritual original, one of those exceedingly rare individuals graced with the courage and vision to venture into the labyrinth of themselves and penetrate the great mystery enshrined at its core. Such a person knows truth for himself, not at second hand, having drunk at the living source.

Afterwards he may teach others, but at once problems arise. Firstly, disciples usually do not possess the spiritual talent of their masters; and secondly, there is a limit to what can be taught anyway, for each individual is unique, an entirely new configuration, and he must in the last analysis find his own way to the centre.

Direct contact with the inspiring presence of a master may allow some to overcome these difficulties. While a teaching (or revelation) is fresh and new there is a special power in it. However, most disciples will settle for being imitators, venerating the master and perhaps becoming good organisers and missionaries able to package and market his teachings very effectively, but always from the standpoint of faith or belief rather than of gnosis (knowledge).

The death of a master will inevitably represent a special crisis. Then his teachings – many, if not most of which were probably designed to meet the needs of ad hoc situations and never intended to be generalised – will be set on a pedestal. They will be formalised and written down. And so in time they will become more or less ossified, lifeless – like flowers set in perspex. Priesthood and hierarchy will assert themselves too, and a worldly structure will orchestrate itself, attracting great wealth and power, which will ineluctably lead to rivalry, schism, careerism, dogmatism and so forth.

All this is *religion* as opposed to what went before, which we might call *spirit*.

Of course, religions do much good. They have given us many of the gifts of civilisation, such as ethics, learning and social structure. But they can also do great harm. Narrow-minded bigotry and intolerance, holy wars and witch-hunts, inquisitions and autos-da-fé are aspects of the dark side of religion. At worst, religion can actively oppose spirit (for the best possible reasons, of course). History is peppered with instances of great mystics, individuals truly inspired by the Divine, being persecuted and even put to death by religious establishments.

Eventually, succumbing to its dark side, a great religion may become more or less completely cut off from the well-springs of its original inspiration. But spirit can never be kept down completely. It will continually reassert itself. If a great religion no longer offers it nourishment, it will go elsewhere. . .

Now, it would be naïve and dishonest to pretend that the religion of Buddhism, as it was developed by other men and women after the death of the Buddha, did not fall into some of the classic pit-falls described above. However, the Buddha himself was very much concerned, not with offering dogmatic formulations, but with helping people to see the Truth and find liberation for themselves.

So, elemental to all his teachings is what we might call a liberal spirit of free inquiry. This spirit is clearly expressed in the *Kalama Sutta*, which describes how the Buddha visited the Kalamas, a clan living in the environs of the city of Kesaputta. After the usual formalities, the Kalamas told him:

> Certain holy men and brahmin priests come to Kesaputta and teach. As for the teachings of others, they mock them. Then others come and do the same thing. As a result, whenever we listen to holy men and priests, we are full of doubt and waver in uncertainty as to who is speaking truth, who falsehood.

The Buddha replied unequivocally:

> Yes, Kalamas, you may well doubt and waver in uncertainty. But do not be misled by report or hearsay or what is stated on the authority of your traditional teachings. Do not be misled by those proficient in quoting scripture, nor by logic or inference, nor after reflection on mere opinion or theory, nor blindly out of a respect for a holy man or priest. *Only when you know for yourselves:* such teachings are good, they cause no harm, they are accepted by the wise, when performed they produce positive benefits and happiness – then, Kalamas, you may accept and abide in them. . .

The crucial words here are *only when you know for yourselves*. . . The Buddha was certainly not trying to peddle the Kalamas just another religion or ideology, however noble. He was not trying to get them to join *his* club. And he was not giving them a set of fixed rules and dogmas, for blind grasping at such things all too easily leads to narrow fundamentalism. He was pointing to something in themselves: a timeless inner centre of wisdom. And with that wisdom invariably goes a warm and kindly compassion for others who are caught in the net of suffering.

For those who need them, all the usual consolations of religion are on offer in Buddhism. One can opt to be a believer, a person of faith and pious devotion. But the main call has always been for the individual to follow the Buddha's example and wake up to knowledge of the Truth for himself (or herself – this is understood throughout), in his own unique way. This is what makes Buddhism so relevent to our times and why it is attracting such a large following in the West today. We Westerners have had enough of organised religion and its products and effects. Right now we need more spirit, more direct knowledge: to drink of the living waters. Indeed we deeply thirst for it.

Shakyamuni Buddha

1 · SHAKYAMUNI BUDDHA

Despite the many developments through which the religious tradition that bears his name has gone, the historical Buddha remains funda-mental. He is the founding genius, the hero, the trail-blazer: the archetypal spiritual seeker who pursues the difficult and daunting quest for liberation to its ultimate conclusion. A kind of Oriental Parzival (but without sword or lance, of course).

Yet, for all that, the Buddha remains a shadowy figure, though Buddhist hagiography has enlarged his life story and embellished it with a baroque complexity of miraculous and marvellous detail. He was apparently born around 566 BCE into a leading family of one of the small tribal republics that had sprung up in northern India. The domains of his people, the Shakyas, were situated right beneath the Himalayan foothills, part of them in what today would fall within the Nepalese Terai. Consequently he is sometimes called Shakyamuni, the 'Sage of the Shakyas'; his personal name was Siddhartha Gautama.

THE EARLY YEARS

Legend has it that soon after Siddhartha was born he was scruti-nised by Asita, a holy man with paranormal powers. Asita foretold that Siddhartha would either become a great world leader or a great religious teacher. This somewhat dismayed the child's father, Shuddhodana, who wanted to see him follow in his own privileged

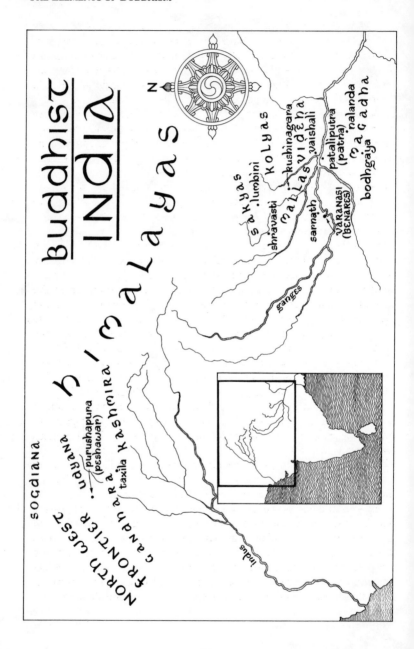

footsteps. Reasoning that it would be experience of the hard side of life that would turn young Siddhartha's mind towards religion, Shuddhodana created a hermetic environment of pleasure and luxury for his son. Consequently the boy grew up knowing little of the realities of life, though by all accounts he was superabundantly gifted with talents and graces, as well as being very high-minded.

In due course, Siddhartha blossomed into a kind of story-book hero and married a beautiful wife, Yashodhara. However, around the time that his one and only son, Rahula, was born, curiosity about conditions in the outside world began to nibble away at him. He was perhaps growing dissatisfied with the mere happiness of life in his marble palace-prisons with their beautiful gardens and pools, bored with the courtesans and dancers and musicians that were laid on at all times to amuse him, tired of lounging around in fine silks and dining on only the daintiest of delicacies.

Shuddhodana responded by arranging for Siddhartha to be driven down to the local village, but he first ordered that all people with any kind of disability be kept out of sight so as not to upset the prince's sensitive nature. The arrangements miscarried, however, for on the first three visits that Siddhartha made to the village he saw things that had a deeply traumatic effect on his over-protected consciousness. He was, in short, summarily initiated into the reality of suffering in three of its most poignant forms: old age, sickness and death. Realising, apparently for the first time, that he too must one day be subject to those fates, he became at once dark and withdrawn. Even in his palaces – *especially* in his palaces – life was no longer tenable.

Then, on a fourth drive to the village, Siddhartha met a sadhu or holy man: one of those ragged ascetics, perhaps with long beard and tangled hair, who still walk the hot and dusty roads of India with no belongings or money, depending on the kindness of other people for their support. Yet this homeless mendicant possessed a certain air of calmness and a nobility of bearing that suggested to Siddhartha that he had come to terms with old age, sickness and death.

So a point of crisis was reached. The outcome was that Siddhartha left his palaces. He gave up wealth and privilege. He even hacked off his handsome jet-black hair and exchanged his fine silk robes for the ragged ones of a holy man. Then he too wandered off into the world, alone and unsupported, to find an answer to the problem of suffering, which would be the same as finding a path to liberation from the painful rounds of cyclic existence. He was then about twenty-nine.

11

THE SPIRITUAL QUEST

Siddartha spent the next six years (536–532) on an intensive spiritual quest. In jungle retreats, he studied first at the feet of Alara Kalama, one of the foremost yogic teachers of his day. Alara taught him methods of deep meditation that led to a very high and subtle dhyana or state of trance. A model student, Siddhartha applied himself wholeheartedly to the practice and achieved realisation. Delighted, Alara offered to promote him to the status of fellow teacher, but Siddhartha declined. This teaching, he reflected, would not lead to total release from suffering but only to protracted sojourn on the Plane of Nothingness. So he went to Udraka Ramaputra, another foremost yogic teacher, and, with similar dedication, absorbed and practised his teachings, only to come finally to the same conclusion as before, only this time the result would be a sojourn on the Plane of Neither Perception nor Non-Perception.

At this point Siddhartha had come to two important realisations. Firstly, he discovered that concentrative meditation (shamatha practice – this is described in greater detail in Chapter 7) does not lead to complete liberation; something else is required. And, secondly, he saw that there inevitably comes a point where teachers can teach us no more. Then, however painful the parting, we have to move on, no longer reaching out to external sources for wisdom but seeking that true source in our own heart centre.

So Siddhartha left Udraka Ramaputra and tried to find his own way. Initially he experimented with extreme ascetic practices: living in graveyards, sleeping on beds of thorns, frying in the noonday heat and freezing beneath the moon at night, he starved and punished his body in the hope that in that way he could root out all desire. Again he applied himself so wholeheartedly that he attracted an admiring circle of five fellow yogis. He also brought himself to the verge of death. Then, at the eleventh hour, terminally weak and emaciated, he realised that he had still not found what he was looking for and would probably die if he persisted. So he abandoned his austerities and took a little food, a lapse that so disgusted the five yogis that they declared, 'Siddhartha has taken to the easy life!' – and promptly abandoned him.

ENLIGHTENMENT

Quite alone now, a man *in extremis*, Siddhartha sat himself on a cushion of kusha grass beneath a peepul tree – the Bo or Bodhi Tree – at a place called Bodhgaya, which lies in the modern Indian state of Bihar. He was determined to sit on that 'immoveable spot' until he found an answer to his problem . . . or die in the attempt.

Siddhartha's spiritual quest reached its climax beneath the Bodhi Tree on the night of the full moon of May. Years before, when as a young boy he had been left beneath a tree during the Ploughing Festival that the Shakyas celebrated each spring, he had closed his eyes and fallen quite naturally into an introverted state of meditation. He now repeated that process and began an in-depth exploration of his own inner being. Much repressed or subconscious material must have 'come up', as modern meditators say: dark fears, erotic fantasies, self-indulgent impulses, fragments of memory . . . but he did not allow himself to be distracted by it. Instead, by watching his own mental movie-show with cool alertness, he was able to neutralise its seductive power and its contents passed away.

Persisting in concentration, his mind became as calm and bright as a mirror, so that he was able to have clear insight into the basic mechanisms that create and sustain Samsara. He relived his own innumerable past births in the different ages of the world – ages of expansion and ages of dark contraction. Then, turning his attention to others, he saw how they circulated through the cycles of birth and death, and that the way in which they passed on was determined by the moral quality of their actions (karma). He then considered how the 'defilements' (sensual desire, ignorance, and so on) that cause suffering could be extirpated and, seeing that it was indeed possible to do so, he was himself freed. He lastly surveyed the twelve links of the chain of Dependent Origination, which in effect describe how birth inevitably leads, by way of a series of predictable stages, to death, which is a prelude to yet another birth – and one that will merely turn the Wheel of Life through another repetitious revolution unless the process is stopped.

Siddhartha must have seen too that he was caught up in this blind, machine-like process himself. If the deep mechanisms of his own being were allowed to have their way, the notion of a separate, individual being or person would inevitably arise – in his case, Siddhartha Gautama – a person with a name, history, social rôle, memories, relationships and so on. But this was really a fictional construct. At depth, in its true nature, the reality was very different. He was not simply Siddhartha Gautama at all, but something far more marvellous than that. His true self was in fact vast, open, unconditioned.

Seeing this, an enormous burden slipped away. He was free at last. For it was the person Siddhartha Gautama who was the prisoner of the gyres of the Wheel of Life, sentenced to endless rounds of suffering. His true self was beyond the dualities of pain and pleasure, space and time, life and death. This was Nirvana.

When, towards dawn, Siddhartha looked up, he saw the morning star rise with new eyes – not the eyes of Siddhartha Gautama but those of the *Buddha*: the 'One Who is Awake', the 'One Who Knows . . . ' This was not merely an event of personal or racial significance but, according to Buddhist hagiography, of cosmic proportions. Some of the more mythically-enriched accounts describe how beings in the heavens and the hells, as though watching from galleries, stalls and auditoria at this momentous event happening at the centre of the world-stage, broke into ecstatic applause. For the Dharma, the Path to Liberation which had been lost for aeons, had been rediscovered. A vast dark age had been brought to an end. New light and hope had entered the world. Others might become Enlightened; some, the pratyeka-buddhas, keep their wisdom to themselves; but it is specifically the function of buddhas, an apostolic line of whom may be traced back into the mists of the beginningless past with vast gulfs between them, to rediscover the Dharma and proclaim it. Siddhartha Gautama is specifically the buddha of our own age.

For some time the Buddha continued to sit beneath the Bo Tree, enjoying the supreme bliss of his Enlightenment. He did consider teaching, but at first he held out little hope that his message would meet with a positive reception. The people of the world were after all very caught up with the idea that they were *persons*, and accordingly spent most of the time securing personal interests, advancing personal ambitions, assuaging personal pains and trying to solve personal problems. Would they be interested in learning that at root they were not *persons* at all: that there was another, more expansive mode of being, one that was free of the suffering that invariably goes with personhood? The Buddha decided not; but then the idea came to him that there might be some with 'just a little dust in their eyes', who might be liberated if they were approached in the right way.

THE TEACHING CAREER

So began a forty-five-year ministry (531–486 BCE) during which the Buddha wandered between the towns, villages and cities of the middle Ganges plain, mainly in the ancient kingdoms of Magadha and Kosala.

From the start he seems to have possessed a kind of radiance that stirred a deep response in those who met him. He was also a teacher of consummate skill and, though he never set himself up as a competitive rival to other religious teachers or to the brahmin priesthood, all the indications are that he was very concerned to get his message across. For one thing, he wished his teachings to be formulated in the local dialects in which they would be fully accessible to ordinary people and not in the rarefied liturgical language of the times. And it is clear from the accounts that large numbers of people, of all classes and conditions, became enlightened by his teachings.

There are many stories relating to this phase of the Buddha's life, but the story of Kisagotami exemplifies as well as any the Buddha's skill as a teacher.

Kisagotami was a poor widow who had suffered many cruel reversals in life. Then, a final twist of the knife, the beloved baby that was all she had in the world died. She was unconsolable and would not have the child's body cremated. Despairing, some of her fellow villagers suggested she go to see the Buddha. She arrived before him, still clutching the child's corpse in her arms. 'Give me some special medicine that will cure my child,' she begged.

The Buddha knew at once that the woman could not take the bald truth, so he thought for a while. Then he said, 'Yes, I can help you. Go and get me three grains of mustard seed. But they have to come from a house in which no death has ever occurred.'

Kisagotami set off with new hope in her heart. But as she went from door to door, she heard one heart-rending tale of bereavement after another. That evening, when she returned to the Buddha, she had learnt that bereavement was not her own personal tragedy but a feature of the human condition – and she had accepted the fact. Sadly, she laid down her dead child's body and bowed to the Buddha.

The Buddha's teachings are not merely for intellectual contemplation. They involve practice: things to do – and things requiring discipline and application. Though many of his early followers were lay-people, there were also those who wished to give up the world and family life in order to devote their time and energy entirely to the Dharma. So emerged the Sangha, the community of Buddhist monks, to which later nuns were admitted. At first the Sangha lived lives of extreme simplicity as homeless mendicants, dressing in rags, living only on alms-food and seeking shelter in caves and beneath the roots of trees. Later, however, thanks to the largesse of wealthy lay benefactors – the Buddha numbered among his devotees kings, aristocrats and rich merchants – they obtained more permanent and comfortable residences during the Monsoon or Rainy Season. These were the beginnings of vihare: Buddhist monasteries.

Such was the purity and power of the Buddha's message that, at first, the Sangha needed no rules to regulate its life. Gradually, however, occasioned by specific lapses, a code of rules, the Pratimoksha, was evolved for monks and nuns; also principles of government, which were highly democratic. The Buddha, it seems, never sought to set himself up as an authority figure or reduce his disciples to the state of blind followers. Nevertheless internal dissension did arise within the Sangha and, on one occasion, the Buddha withdrew in disgust at the quarrelsome antics of some of his monks. The only really serious schism, however, was fomented by his cousin, Devadatta, who naturally comes in for a bad press in the Buddhist scriptures. Devadatta, by all accounts, was a stickler for discipline. He wanted to tighten up the regulations – to, for instance, enforce strict vegetarianism. He also had designs on the Buddha's mantle and, when he failed to have the succession conferred on him, made a number of attempts on the Master's life. All of them failed and Devadatta got his deserved come-uppance, though we know from historical accounts that his followers were still active in India many centuries after the Buddha's death.

THE FINAL YEAR

Comparatively detailed accounts exist of the last year of the Buddha's life. As usual, he wandered from place to place, giving wise and compassionate teachings. He died around 486 BC, when he was about eighty years old, and might have accounted himself lucky, unlike many other great spiritual innovators, to have lived so long. The actual cause of death was some kind of food poisoning that first gave rise to sickness, bleeding and great pain – all borne with characteristic fortitude. His disciples, both monastics and laity, gathered around where he finally lay in a grove of sala trees in Kushinagara, not far from his birth-place at Lumbini. Being human, they were naturally grief-stricken. His last words to them were a pithy encapsulation of his whole teaching:

Impermanent are all created things. Strive on with awareness. . .

Then he passed into Parinirvana, an ineffable state utterly beyond the scope of ordinary mental comprehension or verbal description.

This again was an event of cosmic significance. Great anguish was felt and expressed in all Six Destinations – for a buddha, a fully enlightened one who rediscovers and proclaims the Dharma after it has been lost during a vast dark age, appears in the world only very, very rarely indeed.

2 · INDIAN BUDDHISM

Buddhism has not been a significant religious presence in India for many hundreds of years. But it did thrive in the subcontinent for over 1000 years after the death of its originating genius. During that period it underwent many important developments. With hindsight, we can trace the emergence of three major traditions or new 'turnings of the wheel of the Dharma', each with its own component schools and sects:

1. Basic Buddhism, pejoratively dubbed Hinayana or 'Little Vehicle' by later schools, whose forms, teachings and practices are probably closest to those of the historical Buddha himself.
2. The Mahayana or 'Great Vehicle', which creatively opened up a whole new panoply of approaches to the great project of Enlightenment; and –
3. The Vajrayana or 'Thunderbolt Vehicle', the Tantric path that yet again revitalised Buddhism by introducing special yogic and magico-ritual technologies for securing the goal of Enlightenment.

BASIC BUDDHISM

The Buddha was a dynamic spiritual master teacher who gave out teachings according to the demands of specific situations. Though, by virtue of his attainment, he possessed a certain natural authority, which was apparently quite self-evident (according to accounts he possessed a golden radiance), he never tried to set himself up as a leader figure, nor did he nominate a successor. He obviously wished to inculcate self-reliance in his followers and avoid all the pit-falls that go with power and authority. He just indicated that, if there was a need for guidance after his death, his followers might look to his Dharma, his teachings.

Soon after his death and cremation, however, the Buddha's monks and nuns came together from the farflung regions where they had gravitated and held a great council, the first of several, at which the teachings were orally rehearsed. An 'authorised version' was eventually, but not without some difficulty, agreed upon. It was then committed to memory by specialists and transmitted by word of mouth for more than 400 years. A written version was not produced until the first century CE in Sri Lanka. This huge body of scriptures is called the Pali Canon after its medium, Pali, one of the ancient dead languages of India. An alternative name is Tripitaka (Tipitaka in Pali) or 'Three Baskets', on account of its trivision into three main sections:

1. The Vinaya Pitaka or Basket of Discipline, which includes the code of rules by which monks and nuns should live, plus other materials.
2. The Sutra Pitaka or Basket of Teachings: the collections of long, middle-length, short and other instructional discourses of the Buddha.
3. The Abhidharma Pitaka or Basket of Higher Teachings. The compilers of Abhidharma extracted and systematised the basic philosophical ideas implicit in the Buddha's teachings.

In a way all this repeats a familiar pattern. A great spiritual master emerges, imparts his wisdom to his followers in an ad hoc manner, then goes the way of all flesh. He may even declare, like the great modern sage J. Krishnamurti, that 'there are no teachings' and that 'truth is a trackless land'. But still there always seems an urge to capture and fix the letter of his utterances. Can their spirit, which after all is the heart of the matter, be caught, though? And if there is more reliance on letter than on spirit, is there not a danger of fundamentalism: of applying in life situations not the wisdom of the heart, but hoary precedents enshrined in venerable writ?

In the case of the Pali Canon there are also these matters to consider. The Buddha's original teachings were certainly not given in Pali, or in Sanskrit, the high priestly language of ancient India, but in some other lost demotic language, probably Magadhi, the language of the kingdom of Magadha. They were then retailed by his followers during their missionary activities in other parts of India in a variety of other demotic languages. And moreover, not all those present at the original council agreed with what they heard but held to their own variant versions. Furthermore, during the 400-year oral phase there must have been great latitude for small changes to creep in: insertions and deletions – for the best possible reasons, of course.

So, while it might be tempting to regard parts of the Pali Canon as Buddhavacana, the Word of the Buddha, it would perhaps be a little unwise as well as contrary to the non-fundamentalist spirit of Buddhism to do so. The wisest course would rather be to read and study the scriptures with an open mind, one that is *both* appreciative *and* critical, with a view, not so much to fixing a literal understanding in one's mind, but of imbibing the underlying spirit.

Another historical development after the death of the Buddha was that the Sangha itself was inevitably subject to internal stresses. There had been some dissension during the Buddha's own lifetime, most notably the Devadatta affair, but, with the great unifying and reconciling presence of Shakyamuni gone, difficulties over rules and the interpretation of teachings became more numerous and more difficult to reconcile. There was also agitation against the supremacy of the élite of arhats or monastic elders deemed to have attained Nirvana, who effectively dominated the early Sangha; and assertions of the spiritual rights of less exalted practitioners, including the laity, too.

The long-term result of all this was fragmentation into the so-called Eighteen Schools (actually there were more), including important philosophical schools, such as the Sarvastivada or 'All-Things-Exist' school, whose philosophers put forward a kind of atomic theory, classifying the 'dharmas' or ultimate building blocks of reality, which they believed had same kind of real existence.

By and large, the story during this early period was mainly one of success, and that was in part due to the fact that Buddhism still no doubt retained a great deal of its original impetus and vitality despite all attempts to organise it into a religion. It also enjoyed the patronage of powerful rulers, notably the Emperor Ashoka (third century BCE), who underwent a dramatic conversion after witnessing the terrible carnage produced by one of his campaigns. This transformed him from a conventional war-mongering monarch into an enlightene man of peace, concerned not to enlarge or enrich his Indian empire but to raise the moral standards of his people. It is unclear, however, whether Ashoka actually embraced Buddhism or was just highly sympathetic to it.

MAHAYANA

The Buddha himself foresaw that his teachings would, by stages, lose their vitality and effectiveness. However, by skilfully leaving things flexible and open-ended, he allowed for new waves of creativity and development to periodically revitalise the tradition that he had set going. The first of these was the Mahayana, the so-called 'Great, Vehicle'.

What is the Mahayana? This is not an easy question to answer. The word is really a kind of portmanteau term embracing a whole range of different dispositions and developments that began to arise among the Buddhist faithful a few hundred years after the Buddha's death. These were definitely *Buddhist*; that is, their proponents primarily revered the Buddha and adhered to his basic teachings as well as the goal of Enlightenment. But they also represented the blossoming of hidden potentials that had hitherto lain latent within the tradition. They may have been initiated in one place, but they may equally well have arisen synchronously in different locations at more or less the same time. Various non-Buddhist influences, perhaps even ones from the West, may also have encouraged their emergence.

Over centuries these developments began to be associated with a definite movement whose members consciously thought of themselves as Mahayanists as opposed to their precursors, whom they rather disparagingly dubbed 'Hinayanists'. However, as good and tolerant Buddhists, the followers of both traditions must by and large have understood that they were united in something larger than their differences. So, though some sectarian acrimony and division may have taken place, coexistence was possible. We know from the reports of travellers, for instance, that, even as late as the eighth century CE, both Mahayanists and Hinayanists were living side by side in the same monasteries in India.

Doctrinally, Mahayanists replace the spiritual ideal of the arhat, the 'noble one' who is assured of Enlightenment, with that of the bodhisattva. The orthodox Mahayana view is that the arhat has attained the salvation of Nirvana for his own benefit alone, and has therefore achieved a lesser and, it is hinted, rather selfish goal. By contrast, the bodhisattva is motivated altruistically. He seeks Nirvana, not for himself, but in order to help others. In this respect he is very much like a buddha – and indeed within the Mahayana the concepts of buddha and bodhisattva seem to blur into each other.

The various bhumi or stages on the Bodhisattva Path are fully charted in the Mahayana, as are the concomitant perfected virtues (paramita). The faculty of upaya or 'skill-in-means' is strongly stressed too, for even a bodhisattva prodigally endowed with compassion would be impotent if he lacked the talent for devising effective ways of translating his good-will into practical action. But the paramount Mahayana virtue is compassion (karuna): a warm, even loving concern for others infused with a deep desire to alleviate their suffering. This is elevated alongside wisdom (prajña) as the supreme virtues.

As for the Buddha, in the Mahayana he is seen as the manifestation of a supramundane principle rather than as a flesh-and-blood person. In order to appear as he has in many different realms and times, 'he' has three wonderful bodies at his disposal: 1. the Nirmanakaya, the body in which he appears in the world (though this is not a 'real' body but a magical conjuration for compassionate purposes); 2. the Sambhogakaya, in which he appears in celestial realms to teach bodhisattvas and their ilk; and 3. the Dharmakaya, a kind of cosmic body cognate with the Absolute Dharma, the quintessence of Buddha-qualities, the consummation of Shunyata (Emptiness – see below). The historical Buddha is also now often called Tathagata: he who has realised 'thus-ness' or 'suchness' (tathata).

The Mahayana also spawned a magnificent pantheon of celestial and cosmic buddhas and bodhisattvas, such as Amitabha, the Buddha of Infinite Light, who lives in his Western Paradise of Sukhavati, and Mañjushri, the Bodhisattva of Wisdom, whose adamantine sword slices away false views and delusions (see page 40). Such developments paved the way for new cults of faith and devotion, for pre-Mahayana Buddhism was very much focused in the monasteries and concerned with the heroic struggle for Nirvana by personal effort alone. It was therefore not for the ordinary man but for the educated élite and the dedicated few prepared to renounce the world. Lay people, feeling frustrated or left out, inevitably began to demand a more substantial spiritual status and these new forms were therefore evolved so that they could express simple faith and also, aware of their own limitations, call for help from outside agencies.

At the other end of the spectrum, for the spiritually sophisticated, new trends and schools of philosophy emerged, all of them highly esoteric. These again undoubtedly emerged to meet real needs. Many of the pre-Mahayana schools of philosophy were losing their edge and beginning to deviate, if only slightly, into the swamps and mires of false views. The new wave of Mahayana philosophers therefore set about devising new philosophical methods and systems that would conduce to right views: that is, views consistent with what the Buddha had actually taught. So these were, in a sense, not so much new philosophies as newly-devised upaya or 'skilful means' for arriving at direct perception of old verities. Nor were they systems of pure speculative philosophy as are found in the West but were always linked with meditation practice and so had to point conceptually to the kinds of experience or insight actually gained in the meditation hall.

To get an impression of the vitalising new energy that the Mahayana unleashed, you have only to look at its vast canon of scriptures. Its texts are by-and-large not your everyday book written in plain language and conveying ideas in a logical, coherent form. Rather they are poetically exuberant outpourings from the lofty pinnacle of Enlightenment itself. Amazing things can happen. The reader can be magically transported to the ends of the cosmos, visit infinities of celestial realms encrusted with jewels and suffused with paranormal light, and meet plethoras of buddhas, bodhisattvas and other amazing beings, who perform miraculous feats.

These texts are usually difficult for the modern Westerner to read. True, a few are pithy and to the point; but a great many are lengthy and some, of colossal proportions, are clearly not single works but compilations. Stylistically, there is often much repetition and other devices affording pretext for tedium. We can only deduce that they were not meant to be read as we read books today but were copied, chanted out loud, learnt by heart – and not so much with a view to extracting an understanding of some basic argument but more as devotional acts.

VAJRAYANA OR TANTRA

The traveller in India today can still, in certain religious centres, come across that disturbing kind of sadhu or holy man in whom those perennial irreconcilables, asceticism and eroticism, are brought together. He goes about naked, his body smeared with ashes, his beard and hair long and matted, coloured hieroglyphs daubed on his forehead, and a wild, even crazy look in his eyes. This is a tantrika, an adept of Tantra, it is whispered; he frequents charnel grounds and other macabre places, performing unspeakable rites and practices.

Such holy men are spiritual anarchists. They turn the prudent conventions of orthodox religion on their head. Yet, in tolerant India, it has never ben denied that their Tantric path is a valid one, even though it may not be suitable for all seekers.

When Mahayana Buddhism in its turn began to lose its first vitality, Tantra entered the Buddhist mainstream and stimulated yet another phase of revitalisation and renewal – a third turning of the Wheel of the Dharma. We do not know much about its origins, but by the seventh century CE it had become well established. We now call it Vajrayana[1], the vajra being a Buddhist symbol derived from the mythical thunderbolt of the Indian god Indra: a massive discharge of protean energy that blasts away delusion and inaugurates Enlightenment. It is a very appropriate symbol, for the Tantric path is claimed by its devotees to be a very speedy one, accomplishing in one lifetime what might take countless lifetimes in the Hinayana or Mahayana.

The aim of Tantric practice is to transform one's body, speech and mind into those of a fully-enlightened buddha by special yogic means. To this end a variety of ritual and magical methods have been devised, involving the use of specialised forms such as mandala (symbolic models of the cosmos – see page 83), mantra (sacred formulae) and mudra (hand movements), and accoutrements such as the vajra, the ritual dagger (phurba), the bell (ghanta), and the hand-drum (damaru). The power of such things lies in the fact that, in Tantra, everything is invested with cosmic energy. A simple sound may therefore, by virtue of its inherent quantum charge, produce powerful spiritual effects. Practitioners also work with special deities (known in Tibetan as yidam), which may be benign or wrathful but are always imbued with enlightened qualities.

According to the Tibetan tradition, there are four categories of Tantra: Action Tantra (Kriyatantra), Performance Tantra (Carya-tantra), Yoga Tantra (Yogatantra) and Highest Yoga Tantra (Anut-tarayogatantra). Sometimes Highest Yoga Tantra is divided into three sub-categories; Maha Yoga, Anu Yoga and Ati Yoga, making in all a six-fold scheme. According to HH the Dalai Lama, 'The Highest Yoga set of tantras is superior to the lower ones' and its methods make it faster because 'the mind depends upon the body.'[2] Precisely, the yogi works with the subtle body, through which cosmic energy circulates by way of mystical channels and centres. By reversing the energy, the yogi pacifies the mind.

Tantra has its own arcane texts – a 'tantra' is a scripture – but it places primary importance on the guru. He is the guide who can steer the chela or student through the perilous phantasmagoria of the psycho-spiritual world to the safe shore of Enlightenment. In the eyes of the chela student, the guru should appear equal to the Buddha. Tantra is also veiled in secrecy – this has contributed to much confusion about it – and practice cannot begin without the rite of initiation (abhisheka), when the initiate steps into the mandala of his chosen deity.

As might be surmised from the foregoing, what Tantra brought into Buddhism was practical yogic and magical elements. Magic operates, not with the rational mind, but by invoking less developed but no less powerful strata of the psyche (including the emotions and instincts). Developmental psychologists have, in fact, isolated an evolutionary progression of psychological phases through which the human race has passed on its way to full rationality. In the magical phase, which predominated in the mists of prehistory, the internal and external worlds interpenetrated. Imagined things were just as 'real' as material ones, from which came the proverbial power of mind over matter. Now that the so-called 'higher' phases have been attained, these earlier phases, though neglected, are by no means defunct but can be reawakened and mobilised for work. This is precisely what Tantric yogis actively seek to do.

Without concrete information, one can only imagine that the earliest Buddhists tantrikas were reminiscent of their colourful modern Hindu counterparts or of the devotees of the old Tantric schools of Tibet – that is, siddhas (adepts), rich in 'crazy wisdom', wandering the world alone or with female consorts, or else married yogis who, in addition to their mystic practices, dispensed occult services – divination, exorcism, rain-making and so on – in their localities. Such people may well have represented, as L. O. Gomez has written, 'a radical departure from Buddhist monkish prudery' and 'an attempt to shock the establishment out of self-righteous complacency.'[3] But inevitably, as the Tantric tradition established itself, steps were taken to sanitise and organise it. It was then monasticised and reconciled with orthodox Buddhist philosophy and practice. Eventually integrated systems were evolved which placed the Vajrayana at the apogee of a three-tiered hierarchy and the other traditions of Buddhism – the so-called 'Sutra' traditions – below.

Even today one can hear exponents of reformed Vajrayana declare that their system leads more quickly to a higher realisation than is available in the other traditions. And yet the very thing that gave the Vajrayana its regenerative power – that is, its anarchic quality – has to a large extent been reformed away in the interests of creating a kind of 'safe' Tantra.

But can Tantra ever be 'safe'? Indeed, can authentic spirituality ever be 'safe'? Can it be comfortable and secure and prudently middle class? These are very relevant questions. If we look back to the example of the Buddha himself, we can see that he did not progress spiritually by staying put in his luxurious palaces, enjoying high privilege and status. He had to let go of everything and venture out alone into the great Unknown. He had to confront mystery and danger. His true spiritual heirs, then, are arguably those lone yogis, like the Tibetan Milarepa and some of the early Chinese Zen masters, who went off into remote places to find their own unique ways, rather than those who join institutions and other groupings.

Buddhism gradually went into decline in India after about the seventh century CE. By the thirteenth century it was to all intents and purposes a dead letter. Popular mythology has it that it was the Muslim invasions that destroyed it, or the degenerate influence of Tantra. Yet there were other more significant factors, not least that the ongoing Hindu tradition, with its greater flexibility and involvement with the ordinary life of the people, gained new vitality and reabsorbed much of Buddhism into its own mainstream. Buddhism suffered from being concentrated in the monasteries too, some of which, like Nalanda and Vikramalashila, had grown into great monastic universities where a whole range of spiritual arts and sciences were taught. When the Muslims did attack, the already weakened Buddhists were easily locatable – and 'liquidatable'.

3 · THE BUDDHIST DIASPORA

The decline and fall of Buddhism in India was not the end of the story by any means. Buddhist teachings and practices had already been transmitted far beyond the confines to the subcontinent to places where, coming in contact with new influences and circumstances, they were in time to undergo further revitalising phases of development.

We can trace three principal transmissions:

1. A Southern Transmission that took Buddhism down into many south-east Asian areas falling within the boundaries of the contemporary states of Sri Lanka, Burma, Thailand, Laos, Kampuchea.
2. A Northern Transmission, that took Buddhism up into north and east Asia: into Tibet, China, Mongolia, Korea, Japan, Vietnam and so on; and
3. A Modern Western Transmission, that in the past 100 years has brought Buddhism to Europe (Britain, France, Belgium, Germany, Russia and so on) and North America – and to other parts of the world as well.

THE SOUTHERN TRANSMISSION

Though the Mahayana and Vajrayana were introduced many centuries ago, the brand of Buddhism that nowadays predominates in south-east Asia is the Theravada, literally the 'Way of the Elders', which can trace its origins back to the seminal pre-Mahayana school.

27

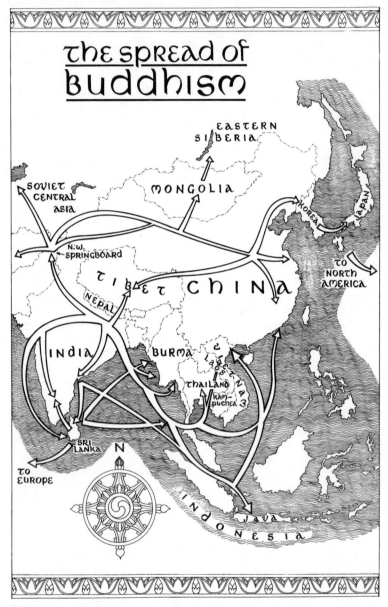

Map showing spread of Buddhism

28

The first successful Buddhist missionary effort was in Sri Lanka. Theravada Buddhism was brought to this gem-like tropical island in the third century CE, by the Emperor Ashoka's own son and daughter, Mahinda and Sanghamitta. Both were ordained members of the Sangha. King Devanampiyatissa received them well, donating a tract of land on which the first of the many monasteries of the island was built. The king, fired with enthusiasm to see Buddhism well-established in his kingdom, was assured by Mahinda that this had been truly achieved when a native-born Sri Lankan was ordained a monk in a sima (consecrated area) on Sri Lankan soil.

Mahayana and Tantric Buddhism later arrived in Sri Lanka, and their devotees came into contention with those of the orthodox Theravada. However, the matter was settled by a council in 1160, which suppressed all non-Theravada schools. Later, Sri Lanka suffered political upheaval due to European colonisation and invasion from south India, and by the mid-eighteenth century its Buddhism was in such a parlous state that bhikshus (monks) had to be imported from elsewhere to maintain the tradition. Revival got under way during the latter part of the nineteenth century, however, generated both by local Buddhists and by European sympathisers, such as the pioneer Theosophists H. S. Olcott and H. P. Blavatsky. A relatively healthy, if rather conservative tradition, with a scholarly bias, currently survives in strife-torn Sri Lanka, but there is also a forest tradition of secluded meditator monks and nuns.

Various forms of Buddhism were also introduced into Burma and, between the eleventh and thirteenth centuries CE, a wonderful Buddhist culture bloomed at Pagan. Because of various schisms and dissensions, however, a 'canonically valid monastic succession' was introduced from Sri Lanka in the fifteenth century, since when Sri Lankan Theravada has been the predominant tradition. During the British occupation (1885–1948), Buddhism became closely associated with Burmese nationalism. Since independence, Burma has been a socialist state – and recently a very troubled one – but Buddhism survives and today Burma is famous for the vigorous meditation methods developed with great success by masters such as Mahasi Sayadaw, U Ba Khin and S. N. Goenka.

Sri Lankan Theravada was established as the predominant tradition in Thailand in the fourteenth century CE. Today Thai Buddhism is highly hierarchic and organised. It also comes under a degree of state supervision and the king is the Supreme Patriarch. Not surprisingly, therefore, the local 'church' has its radicals and reformers as well as its unbending conservatives. Much of its vitality, however, lies away from the cities in rural forest areas where serious practitioners ordain and get down to the business of doing Buddhism. One well-known modern master of the forest tradition is Ajahn Chah, who has trained many Western monks, notably Ajahn Sumedho, the American founder of four new Theravada monasteries in Britain and others elsewhere.

Thai influence has also been responsible for the predominance of Sri Lankan Theravada in Laos and Kampuchea. Tragically, traumatic political strife has decimated the Buddhist traditions of both countries. In Laos, a small remnant of the Sangha is presently trying to work out some accommodation with local Marxism. The position is highly uncertain in Kampuchea, however, where the genocidal Pol Pot of 'Killing Fields' notoriety exterminated the Sangha along with other 'bourgeois' representatives of the old order. Ironically, a glorious Buddhist civilisation flowered a thousand years ago in the Angkor region, under the old Khmer kings.

Indonesia boasts the largest Buddhist monument in south-east Asia: the massive stupa-temple of Borobodur on Java. There is also other evidence that various forms of Buddhism were transmitted to the region in the past but were eclipsed by the coming of Islam in the fifteenth century. Today, however, modest efforts are being made to revive both Theravada and Mahayana Buddhism there.

THE NORTHERN TRANSMISSION

This particular transmission of Buddhism is a saga of high spiritual adventure; yet ironically, though all schools of Buddhism were transmitted, eventually the Mahayana and Vajrayana rather than the orthodox Theravada were to prevail. This in itself must represent a very significant comment on the temperament and cultural inclinations of the peoples of northern and eastern Asia.

The Northern Transmission was constellated and launched from a region which we might call the North West Springboard. It comprised parts of north-west India and modern Pakistan, Afghanistan, Soviet Central Asia and Chinese Sinkiang. This was once a dynamic region through which great trade and migration routes passed, many cultures met and many peoples settled: Tokharians, Kapisans, Soghdians, Bactrian Greeks who came with Alexander the Great; also Kushanas, known in China as the Yueh-chi and in the West as the Indo-Scythians, whose great king, Kanishka, created a mighty empire in the area. One might have expected Kanishka, the Bactrian Greek kings and their kind to have been hostile or at least indifferent to Buddhism. Not so. For a variety of reasons, they were quite prepared to protect and even encourage it. The result was a great flowering, particularly of the Mahayana, and states like Gandhara, situated in the North-west Frontier Region, with Purushapura (modern Peshawar) as its capital, became immortalised in Buddhist myth and legend as places where the Dharma once flourished gloriously. Sadly, all this had been largely swept away by the seventh century CE.

Buddhism reached China in the first century CE from the North West Springboard, carried along the Silk Route by merchants, travellers and Buddhist monks. Small Buddhist groups emerged among expatriate communities in the capital, Loyang, and other cities, and texts began to be translated. The Chinese themselves were apparently resistant to Buddhism at first because their own Confucian tradition preached very different notions, but they were brought around during the Period of Disunity that followed the fall of the Later Han Dynasty. Buddhism, with its teachings on anitya (impermanence) and duhkha (suffering), no doubt offered consolations that the intellectual and aristocratic élite were not able to find in their native traditions during this turbulent and insecure period.

During the Period of Disunity (220–589), Buddhism became actively patronised and encouraged by the foreign dynasties that established themselves in the north; it also found favour in the courts of Han Chinese rulers in the south. Royal blessing and the support of the literati ensured its success. Soon enormous numbers of Chinese were ordaining as monks and nuns – by around 514 CE there were two million of them – marvellous monasteries and temples were built, and the work of translating the scriptures into Chinese was undertaken with great industry. Special 'translation teams' were set up, often headed by a master like the great Kumarajiva, who was brought to China as one of the spoils of war. Popular forms of Buddhism also percolated down to the ordinary folk, who never became exclusively Buddhist but practised the religion alongside the indigenous traditions of Taoism, Confucianism and the folk cults.

Buddhism in China reached its apogee during the Sui and T'ang Dynasties (581–907 CE). The work of importation and assimilation done, a fully Sinicised Buddhism then emerged, forged by the creative interaction of the Indian teachings with local traditions, notably Taoism, and by the Chinese genius itself. Four of the many schools that flourished during this era were distinctly Chinese innovations: Hua-yen, the Avatamsaka or Flower Adornment School; T'ien-t'ai, the White Lotus School; Ching t'u, the Pure Land School; and Ch'an, the Zen school.

The success of Buddhism had caused backlash before, but in 845 the 'church', which now had riches and power enough to eclipse those of the straitened Emperor himself, was subjected to a draconian blow from which it never fully recovered. Buddhism was not actually outlawed, but monks and nuns were required to go back to lay life, monasteries and temples were closed, and monastic lands, slaves and treasuries were seized. The Ch'an and Pure Land schools were resilient enough to survive this holocaust, but thereafter Chinese Buddhism went into an almost fatal decline. True, a thousand years later, in the early part of the present century, efforts were made to regenerate it, often with the help of Western sympathisers, but the Communist Revolution of 1948, and even more so the Cultural Revolution of 1966–76, dealt further savage blows to the already ailing remnant of this once glorious tradition. In the more relaxed climate of the 1980s, Buddhism was accorded a degree of tolerance, monasteries began to function again and people took the robe, though not in large numbers. Any kind of renaissance is highly unlikely while the current Marxist ideologues hold sway but, if it does happen, it will probably be with Western help and encouragement.

China formerly dominated Korea and much of the region comprising modern Vietnam, so Chinese forms of Buddhism were transmitted there. In both regions there were attempts at syncretism. In Vietnam a highly successful blend of Pure Land and Ch'an (Zen) was evolved, while, in Korea, Zen (locally called Son) became predominant, but a Zen blended with Pure Land and other elements. Korean Zen has experienced something of a revival in modern times, but this follows on the heels of some 600 years of decline.

Starting in the sixth century CE, Japan also received the Buddha-dharma, primarily from China. Here again royal favour initially ensured success, the local rulers believing that Buddhism possessed special magical powers that could be invoked to protect both state and dynasty. D.T. Suzuki talks of the Buddhism of the Heian Period (794–1184 CE) being 'flooded with magic ritualism'. The Tantric Shingon school was naturally very popular; also the philosophical Tendai school ('Tendai' being the local equivalent of the Chinese 'T'ien-t'ai'), which evolved its own esoteric ritualism. Buddhism also had to come to terms with the indigenous Shinto cult, whose priesthood initially put up a vigorous resistance. An accommodation between Shinto and Buddhism was, however, successfully forged and lasted down to 1868.

The golden age of Japanese Buddhism was the turbulent Kamakura Period (1185–1333 CE), when the samurai class seized power from the decadent imperial aristocracy and established the Shogunate or military government at Kamakura. The samurai, who were professional fighters, found the teachings of the anti-philosophical, no-nonsense Zen school suited their needs admirably, and adopted it with vigour. Sumurai values and training methods also reciprocally infiltrated Zen monasteries, particularly those of the Rinzai (Lin-chi) school. The other major Japanese Zen school, the Soto (Ts'ao-tung), was also transmitted from China. In addition, devotional cults diffused Buddhism, which had hitherto been very much the preserve of the upper classes, down to the lower orders. Important in this context are the local developments of the Pure Land school, the Jodo-shu and Jodo Shin-shu.

After this fruitful period, Japanese Buddhism lost its creative vigour and a phase of decline set in. Matters were not helped by the fact that important Buddhism centres were broken for political reasons, and the religion was brought under the stifling hand of state control. The Zen tradition again survived best. With the Meiji Restoration (1868), when imperial rule was restored following the demise of the Tokugawa Shogunate, there was another anti-Buddhist backlash, caused by an upsurge of nationalistic feeling and a Shinto revival. But Buddhism was by now strongly rooted enough in Japan not merely to weather the storm but to be galvanised into something of a revival. In modern times, following the trauma of Japan's defeat in World War II, the lay-oriented Nichiren sects, notably Soka Gakkai/Nichiren Sho-shu, have attracted mass followings.

Attempts were made to introduce Chinese Zen Buddhism into Tibet, and indeed a great debate was held at the monastery of Samyé near Lhasa, the capital, somewhere between 792 and 794 CE, when a Chinese Master named Ho-Shang Mahayana spoke up for his brand of Sudden Enlightenment against the gradual approach advocated by the Indian pandit Kamalashila. Kamalashila won and thereafter the Tibetans oriented themselves to Indian Buddhism. In particular the magic and mystery of Tantric Vajrayana appealed to the national temperament, resonating and fruitfully interacting with the indigenous traditions of Bön (originally a death cult) and the animistic folk religions.

We can trace two principal transmissions of Buddhism to Tibet: an initial one begun during the seventh century CE, and a second one starting around the year 1000. The hiatus was caused by a brief but damaging anti-Buddhist persecution launched by a king named Langdarma in the mid-ninth century. This ushered in a dark age during which Tibet fell to pieces politically and Buddhism degenerated. Later, however, a new wave of Buddhist masters came from India, more scriptures were translated and a new wave of development took place that was to last right down to the fulfilment of the Chinese Communist Takeover of Tibet in 1959.

During the first phase (c. 640–838 CE), both monastic and Tantric Buddhism were introduced. Tantra was transmitted principally by an adept named Padmasambhava and still survives in the Nyingma or 'Old' school of Tibetan Buddhism. A beginning was also made on translating Buddhist texts into Tibetan. During the second phase (c. 1000 – 1959), on the other hand, a number of Sarma or 'New' schools established themselves, most of them of the cleaned-up Tantric variety, in which non-Tantric or 'Sutra' elements were integrated with Tantric ones. Better organised than the Nyingma, with strong monastic bases, some of these schools achieved great worldly wealth and power.

We cannot fairly talk of a Tibetan transformation of Buddhism as we can of a Chinese one. To the Tibetans, India was a kind of holy land and the Buddhist teachings that came from there were sacrosanct. After Indian Buddhism had been wiped out, the Tibetans saw themselves as custodians of those hallowed traditions. Yet it cannot be denied that up on the sequestered heights of the Tibetan plateau, effectively cut off from the outside world by formidable geographical barriers, their 1000-year custodianship imbued Vajrayana Buddhism with a new tone and colour. That this was preserved almost intact until the middle of the present century was a kind of miracle, which makes the Chinese decimation of Tibetan Buddhism during the Cultural Revolution (1966–76) all the more poignant.

The Tibetan style of Buddhism spread into Mongolia, parts of China and even into Russia, where it was established among the Buryat people, who before collectivisation grazed their herds and flocks to the east of Lake Baikal in eastern Siberia, and the Kalmucks, who carried it in their migration from Asia to the Lower Volga region. It also reached the Himalayan kingdoms of Bhutan, Sikkim, Nepal and Ladakh. No momentous new developments emerged in any of these areas.

THE WESTERN TRANSMISSION

Buddhist teachings reached the West back in the mists of antiquity, so legend tells us, but significant and lasting connections were not forged until the nineteenth century. Ironically, imperialism was a powerful indirect cause. European administrators, scholars and missionaries working in Oriental colonies began to take an interest in the lost or declining Buddhist traditions, to investigate sites archaeologically, and, having mastered the intricacies of Sanskrit, Pali, Chinese and other languages, to translate texts and study their contents. Only then did the Western world – and the Eastern world too for that matter – become fully aware of the panoramic grandeur of Buddhism.

At the same time, the failure of Western religion to provide real spiritual nourishment, and the growing disillusionment with science and materialistic values, caused many to begin to explore the Eastern religions. Brave new movements emerged, among them Theosophy, an ambitious syncretism devised by a formidable Russian lady named Helena Petrovna Blavatsky. The canons of Theosophy proclaim that the great religions of the world are eroded remnants of a great 'wisdom religion' that once existed and to which Buddhism most closely approximates. Whether they accurately understood Buddhism or not is a moot point, but the early Theosophists usefully commended it to the attention of the Western public, did sterling work in helping to revive the religion in Sri Lanka and elsewhere, and paved the way for the modern Western resurgence.

During the early twentieth century, Western Buddhists gradually began to disentangle themselves from their Theosophical swaddling clothes and started to study the teachings with a view to putting them into practice. Journals went into print, and a few intrepid pioneers took ordination, notably British and German nationals such as Allan Bennett (Ven. Ananda Metteya, ordained 1902) and Anton Gueth (Nyanatiloka Maha Thera, ordained 1904). The trauma of World War I increased interest, and during the inter-war period new societies began to flourish, missionaries from the East arrived (including D.T. Suzuki, 'the man who brought Zen to the West'), and effective propagandists emerged (such as the famous barrister, Christmas Humphreys, and his protégé, Alan Watts).

For some time after World War II, in Britain at least, Buddhism continued to be very much a middle class preserve of intellectuals, artists and professional people. All that was to change dramatically during the 1960s, when enormous numbers of people from all walks of life began to gravitate to Buddhism, particularly young people, who were both disaffected with conventional materialistic values and affluent enough to be able to explore and experiment with alternatives. With the diaspora of lamas after the Chinese takeover of Tibet in 1959, moreover, there was at last access to Tibetan Buddhist teaching, whereas before, Theravada and Zen had been most available and hence most popular. There was also a new commitment to practice, especially to meditation, confirming that the initial, slightly dilettantish phase was over and that a new seriousness had arrived. Ordinations stepped up and, by the early 1980s, Theravada bhikshus (monks) were taking the robe on Western soil, so proving by the Venerable Mahinda's stringent test that Buddhism was well and truly established in this hemisphere.

There has been much high quality Buddhist scholarship in the West, and an enormous number of texts have been published in translation, particularly in English. There is even talk nowadays of the development of a Western 'yana' or vehicle: a Western transformation of Buddhism. On the other hand, it is often pointed out that it took many hundreds of years for a fully Sinicised Buddhism to emerge in China, so perhaps it is too early to talk of such things yet.

Buddhism also reached both the East and the West coasts of the United States during the last century. On the East Coast it attracted the attention of New England intellectuals like H. D. Thoreau and Ralph Waldo Emerson, while on the West Coast Ch'an and Pure Land Buddhism were part of the baggage of the Chinese immigrants who came to work in railway construction or in gold prospecting. Later Japanese immigrants brought their own traditions too. An important milestone was the World Parliament of Religions convened in Chicago in 1893. This brought the Zen master, Soyen Shaku, to the States, and led to his pupil, D.T. Suzuki, spending a number of years working in the USA. Other Zen teachers followed, notably Nyogen Senzaki and Sokei-an Sasaki, with the result that Japanese Zen – there is also now a smidgeon of the Korean variety – became the predominant form of Buddhism. Meanwhile, in Alan Watts, who had emigrated to the States in 1938, receptive Americans, particularly the psychedelic devotees of the Californian Counterculture of the 1960s, found a lucid and persuasive populariser of Buddhist and Taoist ideas. Tibetan lamas began to arrive during the 1960s, and they too found an enthusiastic reception among young Americans.

Today, although there is ample Zen and Tibetan Buddhism, there is very little orthodox Theravada Buddhism in the United States.

There is, however, a new lay movement basing itself on vipashyana (Pali, vipassana) meditation and centring on the Insight Meditation Society at Barre in Massachusetts. Currently, however, the most successful and fashionable Buddhist sect is Nichiren Sho-shu, whose vigorous, this-worldly emphasis and apparently successful chanting practice has won it a mass following, especially in California.

CONTEMPORARY WESTERN TRENDS AND ISSUES

If a distinctly Western 'yana' has not yet appeared, various issues have arisen to which Western Buddhists are going to have to address themselves.

One is the issue of women. Traditionally in Oriental society women are accorded a very subservient rôle and this tendency has fully infiltrated Buddhism. In all Vinaya-based traditions, for instance, a Buddhist nun of many years standing is deemed inferior to a monk ordained for just a few hours. Some Oriental traditions moreover transmit the notion that it is difficult if not impossible for women to become Enlightened; the best they can do is accrue sufficient merit in this lifetime to qualify for a future male rebirth. In the present climate of sexual equality such attitudes raise considerable difficulties.

Another pressing issue is that of social action. Traditionally Buddhists have been socially and politically quiescent – or acquiescent, prepared often to coexist with ruthless régimes. Indeed, until very recently Western concepts like democracy, justice and freedom of expression were largely unknown in the East, where feudal forms of political life predominated. Following this tradition, 'politics' has tended to be regarded as a dirty word in some Western Buddhist circles, as though anything smacking even slightly of it will contaminate the pristine purity of the Dharma. Many Western Buddhists, on the other hand, feel it impossible to turn their backs on such issues as repression, economic exploitation, racism, militarism, environmental destruction and genocide. They have found much inspiration in the life and teachings of the expatriate Vietnamese monk, Thich Nhat Hanh, originator of the term 'Engaged Buddhism', who is now based at Plum Village in France, where he works to alleviate the suffering of his people and to generally promote the cause of peace. Of course, modern Buddhist social activists would want to avoid the old confrontational style of political engagement, with its us-and-them psychology that all too easily leads to bitter and destructive controversy. But equally they are not prepared to sit on

37

their meditation cushions, working out their own salvation however diligently, while the rest of the world suffers.

Finally, as Buddhism develops in the West, it must take cognisance of the distinctive features of the Western psyche, especially individualism and the developed sense of ego (which is not of course to be confused with unreconstructed egotism). Traditional Buddhist schools, because they developed in feudal situations, tended to be based on feudal models. For example, in Japanese Rinzai Zen, the teacher–pupil relationship echoes that of the samurai clan boss and his subservient retainers. There was little scope in such contexts for concepts like independence of thought and action; the individual was a passive unit in a collectivity directed from above. Modern Westerners can only conform to such situations by performing psychological contortions, or else by regressing to a kind of adolescent parent–child stance and thereby avoiding adult responsibility. Real and positive development, therefore, demands that the mature ego be given a place in today's Western Buddhism.

4 · WISDOM 1: THE BASIC TEACHINGS

Buddhist teaching and practice is traditionally broken down into three categories:

1. Shila, or moral restraint;
2. Samadhi, 'concentration', which encompasses a whole gamut of 'spiritual technologies' falling under the general heading of Meditation; and
3. Prajña: wisdom.

All three should be developed more or less simultaneously, for when one advances at the expense of the others there will be imbalance. If, for instance, wisdom is undeveloped or lacking, it may be impossible to understand the insights that arise in meditation, and so, to borrow T.S. Eliot's dictum, 'We may have the experience but miss the meaning.'[1] On the other hand, without meditation, any understanding gained will be just ideas in the mind and hence not fully realised. Finally, without morality one may not have the necessary containing power to handle the very powerful psycho-spiritual energies that may be freed during meditation.

We will look at wisdom first, then morality and finally meditation.

Wisdom is, in a sense, both the beginning of the path and the end, where it assumes an altogether higher or transcendent form.

The wisdom that lies at the beginning is a grasp of the Buddha's

Mañjushri

basic teachings. These are not rigid articles of faith that we have to embrace totally. The Buddha recognised that truth cannot be pinned down once and for all. What held good last week or year is superseded in the changed conditions of today. 'Can you nail down the clouds in the sky, or tie them up with rope?' asks the Zen master. So, in the free spirit of the *Kalama Sutta*, the Buddha's teachings should be regarded as *skilful means* (upaya) for obtaining certain results. We are invited to experiment with them to see if they work for us, in the context of our own everyday lives.

DUHKHA

It was the problem of duhkha, rather than abstract questions like 'Who made the world?' and 'What happens to us after death?', that shocked the Buddha into his own spiritual quest. Duhkha is often translated as 'suffering' but, in fact, it covers a whole spectrum of psycho-emotional states, from a mild sense that things are not quite right to intense physical and mental pain. It may also be taken to mean that there is no lasting peace or rest in life; that we are forever under pressure and subject to disruption. This should *not* be taken to mean, however, that Buddhists believe that life is *all* suffering – a common misconception. The opposite of duhkha, sukha – pleasant feeling – is fully admitted. But pleasure and its ancillaries present us with few problems. Duhkha is problematic, however – and that is why we need to do something about it.

Of course, the human race is endlessly optimistic. It can devise new possibilities for hope, even in the direst circumstances; it can also invent ingenious ways of blanking out the dark or painful side of life. In our own age, with its wall-to-wall entertainment, we have become particularly adept at this. All of which might be applauded as a sign of good spirit . . . if it did not contain an element of wilful blindness: a refusal to see things as they really are – dark as well as light.

The person that desires to have *only* pleasure and refuses pain expends an enormous amount of energy resisting life – and at the same time misses out enormously. He or she is on a self-defeating mission in any case, for just as we evade certain forms of suffering we inevitably fall victim to others. Underlying our glitzy modern consumer culture there is a deep spiritual undernourishment and malaise that manifests all kinds of symptoms: nervous disorders, loneliness, alienation, purposelessness . . .

So blanking out, running away, burying our heads in sand or

videotape will take us nowhere in the long run. If we really want to solve our problems – and the world's problems, for they stem from the same roots – we must open up and accept the reality of suffering with full awareness, as it strikes us, physically, emotionally, mentally, spiritually, in the here-now. Then, strange as it may seem, we reap vast rewards. For suffering has its positive side. From it we derive the experience of *depth*: of the fullness of our humanity. This puts us fully in touch with other people and the rest of the Universe. Suffering can also bring out the full grandeur of our race, its heroic and best potential.

The great American writer, Henry Miller, wrote:

> Only in sorrow and suffering does man draw close to his fellow man; only then, it seems, does his life become beautiful.[2]

I know for myself, though no hero, that the sixteen years I have spent living with leukaemia have put me in touch with life and its true priorities in a very direct way. The disease has helped me face the fear of death, and by making me acutely aware of the extreme precariousness and temporariness of life has at times stripped me of past and present attachments, as well as of plans and projections for the future, all of which make us so tight and inflexible that the vital current of life cannot flow freely through us. Once letting go has taken place, however, the heart opens and, even though one may be in a poor condition clinically, the spirits soar. Other people, sensing this, can be deeply touched too.

If, therefore, we want to live as wholly human beings, we must be prepared to follow the old heroes willingly and consciously into the dark labyrinths and confront the grim denizens that lurk there. All we have to fear is our fear. All we need for protection is courage – and a little wise guidance.

DELUSION AND 'NOT-SELF'

A primary cause of suffering is delusion: our inability, because of a subtly wilful blindness, to see things the way they truly are but instead in a distorted way. The world is in fact a seamless and dynamic unity: a single living organism that is constantly undergoing change. Our minds, however, chop it up into separate, static bits and pieces, which we then try mentally and physically to manipulate.

One of the mind's most dear creations is the idea of the person – and, closest to home, of a very special person which each one of us calls 'I': a separate, enduring ego or self. In a moment, then, the seamless universe is cut in two. There is 'I' – and there is all the rest. That means conflict – and pain, for 'I' cannot control that fathomless vastness against which it is set. It will try, of course, as a flea might pit itself against an elephant, but it is a vain enterprise.

Central to the Buddha's teaching is the doctrine of anatman: 'notself'. This does not deny that the notion of an 'I' works in the everyday world. In fact, we need a solid, stable ego to function in society. However, 'I' is not real in an ultimate sense. It is a 'name': a fictional construct that bears no correspondence to what is really the case. Because of this disjunction all kinds of problems ensue.

Once our minds have constructed the notion of 'I', it becomes our central reference point. We attach to it and identify with it totally. We attempt to advance what appear to be its interests, to defend it against real or apparent threats and menaces. And we look for ego-affirmation at every turn: confirmation that we exist and are valued. The Gordian Knot of preoccupations arising from all this absorbs us exclusively, at times to the point of obsession. This is, however, a narrow and constricted way of being. Though we cannot see it when caught in the convolutions of ego, there is something in us that is larger and deeper: a wholly other way of being.

When I arrived in India in 1971, the Monsoon was in full progress, so I went up to the Himalayan hill station of Mussoorie to escape the excessive humidity of the Plains. By lucky chance, I found hospitable board and lodging in the back room of a small restaurant run by Tibetan refugees. Every day copious cloud boiled up out of the hidden valleys and gorges, obscuring the surrounding foothills. It rained incessantly too. In fact, it was so damp that every morning when I got up my leather belt was rimed with mildew. Nevertheless, though I could see virtually nothing, I always went out walking in the locality.

Then a miraculous transformation occurred. After tea one evening I ventured up to a high rocky vantage-point and found that the Monsoon had suddenly finished. For the first time, there was clarity in every direction. A wonderful sunset was in progress too. The vault of the sky looked as though it has been splashed with the contents of a huge crucible of molten gold. I could also see for what seemed like hundreds of miles across the serried green foothills to where, on the far rim of the horizon, the snowy mountains were catching the light of the setting sun and reflecting it back with redoubled radiance.

Being absorbed in ego identification is like wandering about in Monsoon cloud. Declutching from ego, if only for an instant, is to become aware of an unimagined vastness and beauty that is there all the time but which the blinkers of self-concern prevent us seeing.

SKANDHAS

If the idea of 'I' is a fiction, we may justifiably ask how it arises in the first place. The classic Buddhist answer would run along these lines:

If we take a motor car, for instance, we feel quite sure about what we have. . . until we start taking it apart. But once we have removed the bodywork, stripped down the engine, taken out the gearbox and transmission, removed the wheels and so on – what's left? We don't have a car any more, just a set of spare parts.

It is the same with a person. That too can be stripped down to its basic components, which are traditionally divided into five standard categories: the so-called skandhas or 'groups'. There is 1. the category of the physical, which includes the body and its five senses; 2. that of feeling; 3. perception; 4. mental formations (impulses and emotions); and 5. consciousness or mind. When these groups of components come together in proper working order, the right conditions exist for the illusion of a self and a person to arise. But once they break down and go their separate ways – as at physical death, for instance – then that self or person cannot be found.

What remains is not nothingness, annihilation, however. The Buddha defined that as a wrong view. Nor is it some sort of eternal *something* – another wrong view. There is an elusive 'middle way' transcending both annihilationism and eternalism – in fact all dualities, including life and death. We must seek the truth here.

DHARMAS

In the Abhidharma, the philosophical systematisations of the early Buddhist schools, the search for the ultimate elements of the world-process is taken as far as it will go on the micro level. These ultimate elements are called 'dharmas' – in the Sarvastivadin system there are seventy-five in all – and are said to be insubstantial appearances, in the words of T. Stcherbatsky, 'momentary flashings into the phenomenal world out of an unknown source'. Perpetually in a state of agitation – rather like minuscule Mexican jumping beans, perhaps? – until finally calmed in Nirvana, they are forces rather than substances.

True reality, then, is the dance of these mysterious, evanescent dharmas as they cluster into groups and flow in what appear to be streams (santana). The deluded mind, however, discerns 'things' and 'personalities' here, just as a man looking up into the sky may see the shapes of faces or maps or trees where in fact there are just configurations of cloud; or a thirsty man in a desert may see a lake of cool water which is in fact only a mirage.

The teaching on dharmas – as indeed all the other of the Buddha's teachings – is not meant to be accepted on trust. The dedicated practitioner should actually be able to make his mind so calm, clear and still that he can actually see these infinitesimal 'flashings', of which there are many to the split second. In this way he will once and for all see through the shadow play world of conventional existence and never again be its dupe. Needless to say, of course, only a very gifted meditator practising in ideal circumstances for many years will be able to reach this kind of virtuoso level.

DEPENDENT ORIGINATION

A popular explanation of the way causation works in the cycles of life and death is set out in the teaching of Dependent Origination (Pratitya Samutpada). We have already seen how the Buddha rejected the notion of a Creator God or Prime Mover. All phenomena in the Universe are produced within the cosmos by internal causes. That is to say, each phenomenon is the cause of a further phenomenon, which in its turn will go on to be a cause of. . ., and so on, ad infinitum . . .

Within the life-span of any human being, twelve separate causally active links or 'nidana' may be discerned. There is 1. *ignorance*, that wilful blindness that leads to 2. *volitional action*. Volitional action in turn generates 3. *conditioned consciousness* requiring 4. a vehicle or body (*name-and-form*) to carry it through the world. That body will have 5. doors and windows: the sense organs (the so-called *six bases* – that is, the five senses plus mind) upon which stimuli will impinge, thereby creating 6. *sense impressions*, which in their turn will generate 7. *feelings* that lead to 8. *desire*. Desire is a kind of intoxicant that makes us blindly cling to whatever we find desirable (and of course reject what we find repulsive). So 9. *attachment* is created, and that in turn triggers 10. *becoming*, from which comes

11. *birth* – and birth, as the Buddha never tired of ephasising, inexorably produces 12. *old age, death* – and indeed all the ten thousand ills and sorrows that flesh is heir to.

This sounds difficult, but we have similar ideas in the West. The saying, 'One thing leads to another', is in fact a pithy summary of Dependent Origination!

But let us take a loose example. A young man sees a shiny sports car. It inspires strong feelings in him – he imagines the elation as he drives down the road at 100 m.p.h. with the hood down, the wind streaming through his hair, a pretty girl beside him. Desire is born: he wants to possess the car. So he borrows the money to buy it. Once he has it, his life changes. He has to work harder in order to run and maintain the car – and to pay back his debt. It is a struggle, but he is so attached to the car that he cannot bear the idea of losing it. Things get difficult, so he takes on extra work. Gradually stress and overwork undermine his health. He falls ill with a kidney complaint. A few years later he dies, which in due course occasions a new birth. All this happened, the Buddhist explanation would run, because he was deluded: he thought that true fulfilment lay in getting that sports car, whereas in fact doing so merely led to a series of escalating complications. The rebirth resulting from his death will merely repeat a similar process. . . until the lesson is learnt and a firm resolution arises to seek escape from the endless cycles of old mistakes.

KARMA

What force couples each link in the chain of Dependent Origination, keeping the Wheel of Life in perpetual spin? The answer is *karma*. The word – karman is in fact the correct Sanskrit form – has now penetrated the Western consciousness, though, from the Buddhist point of view at least, in somewhat distorted guise. It is often called the Law of Cause and Effect, so it is about the consequences of actions of body, speech and mind. And consequences are very important in Buddhism.

Any action that is willed, however subtly, by the person who performs it will always produce a future 'ripening' and ultimately a 'fruit' of similar moral quality, because in the human sphere karma operates in an ethical manner. So an unethical action will induce a come-back of like kind in this life or some future rebirth; and the same goes for morally good or indifferent actions that are willed and freely undertaken. In the Bible it says something similar: that we reap what we sow. If we want to progress spiritually – or even just to live with minimum aggravation – it therefore behoves us to to be very careful how we speak and act, for there is no way we can escape the consequences. As it says in the *Dhammapada*, a concise and poetic early Buddhist text:

> If a man speaks or acts with an impure mind, pain pursues him,
> even as the wheel follows the ox that draws the cart.[3]

This teaching should not be used as a pretext for unkind judgementalism, however. For instance, were someone to fall ill, a censorious person might declare, 'Ah well, that's the result of past karma. He's merely reaping what he sowed.' This, however, is to ignore the fact that non-karmic forces are also in play. Our bodies, being organic, are subject to growth and decay regardless of how we behave. Various circumstantial factors also have a bearing on how things turn out. In any case, who is it that performs an action? If ego is ultimately an illusion, there is no doer, just the deed. Where then does moral responsibility lie?

Moreover, nowadays scientists are discovering that laws – and, in Buddhist terms, karma is a law – only work up to a certain point. Beyond that anything – literally *anything* – can happen. So indeterminacy or uncertainty is built into the basic workings of the Universe. The Buddha himself may have been implying something like this when he rebuked his loyal attendant, Ananda, for saying that he fully understood karma.

REBIRTH AND DEATH

As must have become quite clear by now, Buddhism does not hold with nihilistic views of death. There is no yawning abyss of pure nothingness into which we finally disappear. There is just Samsara, the cyclic world-process – and escape from it.

Buddhists are often thought to subscribe to the idea of reincarnation. This is not strictly true. Reincarnation presupposes that some kind of enduring soul or essence, something with unchanging personal imprints, commutes from body to body down through the marches of time. As we have seen, however, the Buddha denied the existence of any soul that might reincarnate. What he did admit of was something slightly different, which we might call *rebirth*. This maintains that there is a *causal connection* between one life and a subsequent one. Nothing is handed on in the transaction, however; the following life is a completely new one. But the form it takes is conditioned by the previous one. It is rather like a billiard ball flying across the green baize of a billiard table. It hits another ball and that canons on at a speed and in a direction that owes something to the first ball (and also to other incidental factors), but it does not take away anything material or essential from the first ball. Another analogy is of the transmission of a flame from one candle to another.

Strictly-speaking, we die and are reborn from moment to moment. This may seem a little far-fetched at first, but if one were to look at two photographs of the same person, taken, say, twenty or thirty years apart, would one see the same person, the same face and body, the same look in the eyes? Or would all those things – and also unseen things, such as attitudes, beliefs and emotional and mental states – be very different? The answer is self-evident.

Physical death, however, is undeniably a more obvious and disturbing 'death' than the smaller ones that happen from moment to moment. In Tibetan Buddhism we find a detailed analysis of the states that arise in the 'bardo' or intermediate state that intervenes between one life and another. The bardo is a terrifying phantasmagoria in which all kinds of spectres, gods, demons and other apparitions loom up before the bewildered disembodied consciousness[4] traversing it. Wonderful 'luminosities' appear too, the first of which is the true Dharmakaya (see page 22) wherein lies liberation, but the consciousness traversing the bardo will usually be too confused to see them for what they are and will instead be swept onwards towards rebirth, which will take place within a maximum period of forty-nine days. If a human rebirth is to take place, the future parents will be seen making love, lust will arise and the consciousness will try to interpose itself but find its way barred. The annoyance it then feels will be the seal of its conception.

The odds in favour of a human rebirth, from where alone escape from Samsara is possible, are said to be very slender. If a blind turtle swimming in a vast ocean came up for air once every one hundred years, what would be the likelihood of it putting its head through a golden yoke floating on the surface? So, if we are favoured with a 'precious human rebirth', we should take care to put it to good use in the interests of achieving liberation, otherwise we may be dispatched to the other grim 'destinations' – the hell realms, the realm of the hungry ghosts and so forth – and circulated there for aeons before we get another chance.

CHANGE AND IMPERMANENCE

The Buddha stressed the dynamic nature of existence. This resonates with the ideas of some early Greek philosophers, such as Heraclitus, who maintained that 'All is flux' and 'You can't step into the same river twice.'

Now, all this sounds like common sense. Yet there is something about our minds and emotions that kicks against the idea of change. We are forever trying break the dynamic world-dance, which is a unity, into separate 'things', which we then freeze in the ice of thought. But the world-dance doggedly refuses to remain fragmented and frozen. It swirls on, changing from moment to moment, laughing at all our pitiful attempts to organise and control it.

In order to live skilfully, in harmony with the dynamic Universe, it is essential to accept the reality of change and impermanence. The wise person therefore travels lightly, with a minimum of clutter, maintaining the proverbial 'open mind' in all situations, for he or she knows that tomorrow's reality will not be the same as today's. He or she will also have learnt the divine art of letting go – which means not being attached to people and possessions and situations, but rather, when the time for parting comes, allowing that to happen graciously.

In his classic work, *Walden*, the nineteenth century American writer H.D. Thoreau writes amusingly but perceptively of many of his fellow New Englanders 'well nigh crushed and smothered' under the load of their property, including 'a barn seventy-five feet by forty, its Augean stables never cleansed, and one hundred acres of land, tillage, mowing, pasture and wood lot!'[5] How much more agony, then, does our attachment to relationships – to friends and loved ones – cause us.

Looking back, I realise that this fact of change/impermanence struck me forcibly many years ago, before I ever studied or practised Buddhism. One afternoon I was standing at the window of the first-floor flat I occupied when I was a student, watching the people coming and going in the street below. A woman came along, pushing a pram up the hill. There was nothing particularly striking about her. She looked like any slightly harassed young mother, a little negligent of her appearance, probably quickly popping out between chores to pick up a few things in the shops. With slow amazement, however, I began to recognise something familiar about her. She was someone with whom I had had a brief relationship some years before. Then everything had been utterly different. She was eighteen, had just left home to start her first year at university, and was not just very pretty but radiated that love of life a girl can have at that age, when the world seems a bountiful cornucopia. I could even remember the first time that I had seen her. Her face, especially her bright smile, were impressed on my memory, as in a sharp colour photograph. . . Beauty, then, was not a possession, something that could last. It was an event – and a very brief one. The woman in the street was not the girl I had loved. She was someone else, someone different.

DESIRE

If the basic project of mainstream Buddhist practice is to unmask the ego illusion for what it is, one of the main prongs of attack is directed against desire. Desire gets a very bad press in the Buddhist scriptures. It is a poison, a disease, a madness. There is no living in a body that is subject to desire, for it is like a blazing house.

Now, desire lives and grows by being indulged. When not indulged by the application of ethical restraint and awareness, on the other hand, it stablilises and begins to diminish, though this is not an easy or comfortable process, for the old urges clamour for satisfaction for a long time.

This kind of practice, of course, cuts directly against the main currents of modern consumer society, where desire is energetically encouraged and refined to new pitches and variations by the powerful agencies of marketing and publicity. But it also cuts against the more moderate desires – for family, wealth, sense-pleasures and so on – sanctioned in simpler, more traditional societies, including the one into which the Buddha was born. We can never be at peace while desire is nagging at us.

The flip-side of desire is aversion, a pushing away of that which we dislike as opposed to a grasping onto things we like. Aversion too must be put to rest.

Desire, aversion and their bedfellow, delusion, are the basic faults or frailties of character that drive us through the painful cycles of Samsara. They are symbolically represented at the very hub of the Wheel of Life by a cock, snake and pig, all chasing each other and biting each others' tails in an unbreakable circular chain.

HIGHER QUALITIES AND VIRTUES

Through taking the medicine that the wise doctor, the Buddha, prescribes – that is, through regular, balanced practice, usually over a fairly extensive period of time – many of the complicated problems that arise in life sort themselves out quite organically. Time and energy are at the same time freed for actively inculcating moral qualities such as patience, kindness, resolution, sympathetic joy for the successes of others, compassion for their suffering, and so forth. There is also more latitude for study and meditation.

As practice deepens over time, more specialised qualities will arise, including the higher form of wisdom we mentioned earlier. This enables the practitioner to see things as they really are, clearly, no longer through the distorting lenses of desire-based fantasy, projection and so forth.

As the process proceeds towards its culmination, detachment from both the world and the self advances. The clamour of urges within, the ripening of old karmic seeds, dies away until finally the practitioner is capable of such dispassionate acceptance of all the vicissitudes of life that even death ceases to frighten him.

There is a traditional story that once a rebel army swept into a town in Korea and all the monks of the local Zen Buddhist temple at once fled except for the abbot. The rebel general swaggered into the temple and was annoyed when the abbot did not immediately prostrate before him.

'Don't you know,' he roared, 'that you are looking at a man who could run you through without blinking?'

'And you,' replied the abbot, 'are looking at a man who can be run through without blinking!'

The general was taken aback. After a moment, he bowed respectfully and retired.[6]

Or, as the great modern Irish poet, W.B. Yeats, wrote in his own epitaph:

> Cast a cold eye
> On life, on death
> – Horseman, pass by. . .[7]

NIRVANA

The end of the path is likened in the early scriptures to the blowing out of a candle when there ceases to be fuel to keep it alight. This is Nirvana. Identification with a self has ceased; indeed all urge to exist as a person – or to exist at all – has ceased. Desire and aversion have been pacified. Delusion has been replaced by clarity. At the micro level, the agitation of the dharmas has completely calmed down. Cyclic existence, birth and death, are transcended.

We must be careful not to reify this as sheer nothingness – or as a super transcendental something. It is beyond birth and death, existence and non-existence – and utterly beyond the power of the mind to know or of words to tell. We are assured, however, that it is the greatest bliss. Life in the body may still continue, and teaching may take place too – as in the case of the Buddha – but, ultimately, there is a further and equally ineffable transition at physical death. This is Parinirvana. Of the Buddha's own final passing or Parinirvana, it is written:

> As a flame blown out by the wind
> Goes to rest and cannot be defined,
> So the wise man freed from individuality
> Goes to rest and cannot be defined.
> Gone beyond all images –
> Gone beyond the power of words.[8]

5 · WISDOM 2: MAHAYANA DEVELOPMENTS

As the Buddha said that all things were subject to change, it was quite consistent with basic principles that later generations of Buddhists should modify, restate and develop his teachings. In this chapter we will look at the most important developments that took place after the rise of the Mahayana. I want particularly to examine the reformulations of the anatman teaching, which many regard as the key teaching that distinguishes Buddhism from other Indian religious systems.

We tend today, of course, to separate Buddhism from the other Indian traditions, as though it had an autonomous life of its own. Actually it was very much an integral part of 'the philosophical laboratory which was the India of [the Buddha's] time' (T. Stcherbatsky) – and indeed continued to be for over a millennium afterwards. Buddhist thought and practice influenced and in turn were influenced by those of other non-Buddhist Indian schools.

The anatman teaching was originally very much a reaction against the notion of atman, which is quite central to mainstream brahmanical religion. There is, so brahmins and rishis believe, an Ultimate Reality or Self that they call Brahman, which can be found, not in some heavenly sphere, but in the heart of man, in which case it is called atman or the self. Actually there is no difference between Brahman and atman. The Self and the self are one.

The great rishis and yogis of the *Upanishads* stressed the unknowable nature of Brahman/atman. The best that they could do was to describe it in negative terms: *Neti, neti* ('Not this, not this'). The problem is, of course, that the thinking mind cannot let things rest. It will always conspire to trap them in the net of thought and describe them through the medium of words – even when warned not to do so. So gradually the idea of atman began to degenerate. Images and ideas and verbiage were projected onto the blank screen of that great mystery – until it was a mystery no more.

The Buddha's mission was therefore essentially a reformist one. He wanted to purify atman of all those projections and restore its unknowableness. So, when he taught anatman, he was not asserting that there is no atman, no self (and hence no Self – no Ultimate Reality), as indeed many Buddhists have thought. *Rather he meant that anything you think or say about atman is not atman.* Atman is beyond all words and ideas. You cannot grasp it with the thinking mind. But perhaps you can purify and open yourself in order that it can fill you. Then you can be it.

Even the Buddha's formulation of the anatman doctrine, then, insofar as it is itself verbal-conceptual, cannot be perfect or definitive. Not surprisingly, therefore, not long after his death, during the period when the Eighteen pre-Mahayana Schools flourished in India, slight distortions of the teaching began to creep in. It had probably begun to lose vitality too. With the rise of the Mahayana, therefore, new attempts were made to revitalise and restore the teaching to its original purity. In the process, as we shall see, the whole thing goes through a 180 degree shift, from negative formulations to more positive ones.

Indeed, we can trace shifts within the Buddha's own presentation. For instance, in *The Greater Sutta on the Destruction of Craving*[1] the Buddha sharply disabuses Sati, the fisherman's son, of the notion that 'consciousness (viññana), not anything else, continues through life and from life to life,' this consciousness being 'what speaks and what feels and experiences the fruits of karma, good and bad.' The truth, the Buddha maintains, is that consciousness only arises in dependence upon the 'bases of consciousness' (ayatanas). Visual consciousness, for instance, only arises in conjunction with the sense of sight and visible objects. In the *Brahmajala Sutta*[2], on the other hand, the Buddha talks of 'viññanam anidassanam anantam sabbato pabham' ('consciousness which is characterless, unending, everywhere shining'). So in one case he seems to be denying that Ultimate Reality is pure consciousness, whereas in the second he appears to be admitting just that. Also, in the *Udana*, he talks positively of an 'Unborn, Unbecome, Unmade, Unconditioned', without which there would be no escape from all that is born, become, made and conditioned.

It would be wrong to see these things as simple inconsistencies. As the Buddha was a pragmatic teacher, his pronouncements were not meant to be definitive statements of truth but, rather, were shaped to suit the needs of the moment and the individuals that he was addressing. Sati was probably rather stuck on the idea that consciousness was Reality. The Buddha merely wanted to open his mind up again.

SHUNYATA

With the rise of the Mahayana, we find the Anatman Teaching reformulated in the concept of Shunyata ('Emptiness')[3]. This Emptiness is not pure nothingness, of course; nor is it a kind of transcendental something. Rather it is a medicine to remedy the compulsive illusion-making habits of our minds, particularly their tendency to think of persons and things as separate, self-created and self-sustaining.

Shunyata indicates, therefore, not the presence of something but rather a resounding lack or void, specifically a lack of inherent existence or 'own nature' (svabhava). This goes as much for dharmas, those ultimate essences of the world-process, as it does for people and things. In Abhidharma there is a general tendency to think that dharmas are somehow real, though not to the extent of possessing atman. In the Mahayana, however, dharmas are decreed unequivocally to be empty, along with everything else. Even Emptiness is ultimately empty!

THE BODHISATTVA AND HIS COMPASSION

As well as dissipating delusion, an understanding of Shunyata is said to produce a deep compassion (karuna) for the suffering of sentient beings. Compassion means 'to suffer with' – to actually share and feel the sufferings of others as though they are one's own. Obviously a breaking-down of those psychological boundaries that divide 'I' from others has taken place here. In Mahayana teaching, compassion is thought to lead to a deep resolve to fulfil the goals of the spiritual life in order to help others to become free – particularly free from suffering. This is technically called bodhicitta ('Enlightenment mind') and its presence elevates a person to the status of a bodhisattva ('Enlightenment being').

To become a bodhisattva one must already be well-advanced along the path. One must have fully understood the Buddha's teachings on karma and rebirth, Dependent Origination and so forth, had insight into Emptiness and felt the stirrings of deep compassion. In some texts, it is stated that some advanced bodhisattvas have actually attained Enlightenment; that is they are buddhas, no less. In others, however, it is suggested that they 'postpone' their own Enlightenment. Mostly, however, the term is clearly meant to signify someone who is a buddha-in-the-making, motivated altruistically rather than selfishly.

A fine impression of what it practically means to try to live the bodhisattva life is given by the Indian teacher Shantideva in his classic poem, *Bodhisattvacharyavatara* ('Guide to the Bodhisattva's Way of Life')[4]. An enormously high degree of idealism and earnestness is required, such as one would expect to find extremely rarely, if at all, in our contemporary world.

To begin with, Shantideva is smitten with horror at the dire implications of life in Samsara. At any moment, one can be led away to the torture chamber or struck down with disease. The body is 'like an object on loan for but a minute', and when the 'frightful messengers of death' call, which can be at any second, it avails one nothing to have riches, reputation or loved ones. One quits this existence utterly naked and alone.

'Who can afford me real protection from this great horror?' he cries with very real anguish.

There is real protection . . . and a way of salvation – the way of the bodhisattva, in which resides an 'ocean of virtues'. Shantideva determines to follow it and be the doctor, medicine and nurse 'for all sick beings in the world until everyone is healed.' Thus bodhicitta (see page 55) is awakened and, seeing that a selfish orientation, far from achieving the happiness and satisfaction it seeks, merely perpetuates suffering, he surrenders it. Repenting wholeheartedly of all his former sins, he determines to bind the crazy elephant of the mind. For there is 'nothing to fear but the mind'; it is the origin and source of all evil actions that cause hellish suffering. He will therefore examine his mind before doing or saying anything and, if he finds his motivation tainted, will 'remain like a piece of wood'.

He will also be open and at times 'be the pupil of everyone' – excellent advice! Conscious too that one moment of anger can destroy the good generated by wholesome deeds performed 'over a thousand aeons', he will practise patience. If someone hurts him, he will reflect that this is just the ripening of his own past karma, and bear no malice. Indeed he will 'be happy to have an enemy', for it affords opportunity to practise patience and so assists his practice. He will also restrain his sexual passions.

The bodhisattva will consciously develop enthusiasm to counter any disposition to laziness that might impair his practice. Then, 'by seeing the equality of self and others' he will give up all 'self-cherishing' and 'practise that holy secret: the exchanging of self for others'. He will actually conceive of others as 'I', as his own self, their bodies as his body, and take to himself their suffering – though, of course, through his mastery of wisdom ('those who wish to pacify suffering should generate . . . wisdom,' he tells us, devoting a whole chapter to the subject), he knows that in the final analysis there is no 'I', hence no owner of suffering. Building up his generosity, he will also give everything away, even his own flesh. And all this will be done, not out of some drab sense of duty, but with actual joy. He can never do enough for others. He would even enter the deepest hell to alleviate their pains.

Finally, in true bodhisattva style, Shantideva dedicates all merit (good karma) that might accrue to him to the liberation of all beings everywhere, and hopes that they will 'obtain an ocean of happiness and joy'. For the true bodhisattva's compassion is never limited a few chosen beneficiaries. It goes out equally to the whole world, like the warmth of the sun. The same qualities of goodwill, friendliness and harmlessness are bestowed upon all, without distinction, 'as if they were his mother, father, son or daughter'.

THE BODHISATTVA PATH AND ITS PERFECTIONS

The bodhisattva cultivates specific virtues to perfection. There are six or sometimes ten of these 'paramita': 1. dana (giving); 2. shila (morality); 3. kshanti (patience); 4. virya (effort); 5. dhyana (meditation); 6. prajña (wisdom); 7. upaya (skill-in-means); 8. pranidhana (resolution); 9. bala (strength); and 10. jñana (knowledge).

The development of these virtues corresponds to a ten-stage Bodhisattva Path. As set out in the *Dashabhumika Sutra*, the stages are called 1. Pramudita (the Joyful); 2. Vimala (Purity); 3. Prabhakari (Refulgence); 4. Arcishmati (Blazing); 5. Sudurjaya (Difficult to Conquer); 6. Abhimukhti (Presence); 7. Duramgama (Far Going – beyond this stage it is not possible to 'backslide'); 8. Acala (Immoveable) 9. Sadhumati (Good Mind); and 10. Dharmamegha (Cloud of the Dharma), the very apotheosis of bodhisattvahood, where they will protect and enlighten all beings, be omniscient, 'lords of the ten powers', and so on.

THE ABSOLUTE AND THE RELATIVE

Mahayana teachers do not deny that there is a conventional world, only that this world is not what we usually take it to be; that is, real (permanent, self-sustaining, containing separate entities, and so on). This world has its own truth too, but it is a relative truth that is by its very nature compromised, not perfect. There is another frame of reference which is not compromised, however. It accurately reflects reality. The absolute truth that obtains here is called paramartha satya. Worldly or relative truth is called samvriti satya. We could call them profound truth and superficial truth. They correspond to two perspectives: the transcendental (lokottara) and the worldly or relative (laukika).

PRAJÑAPARAMITA

The first major Mahayana teaching to emerge was the Prajñaparamita or 'Perfection of Wisdom' (the so-called 'Wisdom that Has Gone Beyond'). Here we find a number of difficult texts of varying length. One very brief one, for instance, maintains that the whole teaching can be summed up in the letter A (Skt. Ah). Another takes 100,000 verses to present it. The *Heart Sutra* and the *Diamond Sutra* are the most well-known and among the most concise texts.

All the texts are declaimed from the lokottara or transcendental point of view. That is, from a position of absolute non-duality, beyond all discriminative thought and verbal constructions. Viewed from this sublime vantage-point, which is really no different from that of Enlightenment itself, there is no Buddha and no Enlightenment, no defilements and no purification, no production (of dharmas) and no extinction, no karma and no consequences of karma. There are no beings to be saved, therefore no bodhisattvas to save them. Form merges with emptiness, Samsara with Nirvana.

How can such things be? Well, the Buddha could not think 'I am the Buddha', for instance, for that would mean he had in his mind the idea of a person who possessed buddhahood. Being a buddha, he is at one with buddhahood; there is no duality. Therefore, for the Buddha there is no Buddha. Likewise 'Enlightenment' is an idea that only occurs to those who are not Enlightened. Indeed, they are a long way from it. It is 'those who do not consider whether they are far from Enlightenment, or near it' who are truly on course. And again, 'Nirvana' and 'Samsara' are only concepts in the minds of those who discriminate. For those who do not discriminate (that is, buddhas and bodhisattvas) 'Samsara and Nirvana become exactly the same . . .'

So all terms, including spiritually prestigious ones like 'buddha', 'Enlightenment', 'bodhisattva', 'karma' and 'dharma', are just conventional constructions. Buddhas and bodhisattvas use them as skilful means to help suffering beings – though of course in an ultimate sense there are no beings and no suffering. Thus buddhas and bodhisattvas regard those whom they help as no more real than an army of phantoms conjured up by a skilful magician.

What then is the Prajñaparamita mode like? It can be compared, the texts say, to the vacuity and purity of space. The buddhas and bodhisattvas who 'course in it' take their stand nowhere and in nothing, neither in the conditioned nor the unconditioned. They seek no psychological supports, yet their position is diamond-solid. It will not crumble like Samsara and all its creations. For Samsara, it is continually emphasised, 'has no inner core':

> As stars, a fault of vision, as a lamp,
> A mock show, dew drops, or a bubble,
> A dream, a lightning flash, or cloud,
> So should one view what is conditioned.[5]

The Prajñaparamita exults in its own transcendental perspective and brings it poetically alive, while at the same time conspiring to strip us of all affirmations, all mental/verbal constructions, and drive us into the arms of that marvellous Beyond.

MADHYAMAKA

Tradition has it that the amorphous teachings of the Prajñaparamita were systematised by a sage named Nagarjuna (second century CE), the seminal master of the Madhyamaka or 'Middle Way' School. Highly celebrated, he is sometimes characterised as a second Buddha.

Though some have disputed his historicity, hagiography has it that Nagarjuna came from south Indian brahmin stock. He initially mastered magic, which he successfully used to make himself invisible so that he could seduce the women in the local palace. However, when three of his cronies were caught and executed, the perils of lust were forcibly brought home to him and he hastily embarked on Hinayana Buddhist training. Later he graduated to the Mahayana. One source maintains that he received instruction from the nagas, a species of divine cobra that lived at the bottom of the sea. This may figuratively mean that he was the author of an important new teaching; or the word 'Naga' may simply have been the name of a south Indian tribe. He subsequently wrote texts, notably the *Mulamadhyamaka-karika* ('Middle Way Verses'); there are suggestions too that he was responsible for the composition of some Prajñaparamita texts. He masterfully championed the Mahayana in open debate with the devotees of other Buddhist and Hindu schools, like the Samkhya, Vaishesika and Nyaya. Highly venerated, he spent his later years in a monastery built for him by a patron-king, and ended his life by his own hand. His chief disciple was another south Indian brahmin named Aryadeva.

Nagarjuna brought to Mahayana Buddhism, not some creative new philosophical position, but a critical method that, if properly applied, would expunge all views and opinions by showing their ultimate absurdity, thereby at once restoring the mind to its native Prajñaparamita mode, free of all dualistic thought formations. As he himself says at the conclusion of the *Mulamadhyamaka-karika*: 'I reverently bow to the Buddha who, out of compassion, has taught the true doctrine *in order to relinquish all views*.' So this is a philosophy that arrives at no conclusions. It in fact puts an end to all speculation and rumination – or, put another way, it probes the ultimate limits of what can be meaningfully thought and said. In this respect it resonates with the modern linguistic philosophy of Ludwig Wittgenstein.

Nagarjuna's method is described as dialectical: that is, it exploits the quirky, dualistic nature of language to turn all propositions on their heads. He uses various devices to this end, notably his famous tetralemma, by which a simple proposition may be reduced to four logical forms: 1. A; 2. not-A; 3. both A and not-A; and 4. neither A nor not-A. To take a concrete example: 1. Everything is real; 2. Everything is unreal; 3. Everything is both real and unreal; and 4. Everything is not real and not unreal.

Nagarjuna also draws a parallel between Shunyata (Emptiness) and Pratitya Samutpada (Dependent Origination). In his view, the importance of the latter is that it points up the dependence or relativity of all things in the conventional world. They are like the parts of a cathedral, all helping to maintain and support each other, so that if one is taken away the whole structure will collapse. Seeing dependence and relativity in this way is to see Shunyata and be thereby liberated. This liberation depends, then, upon a change of perception and knowledge, nothing more. The world does not become another world, for there is no separation between Samsara and Nirvana – 'the limit of Samsara is the limit of Nirvana'.

The influence of Nagarjuna and his school was enormous. Stringent Madhyamaka became the dominant philosophy in Tibet and remained so down to the time of the Communist takeover in 1959. It was also successfully transmitted to both China and Japan, and is at present being enthusiastically studied in the West.

YOGACARA

Although Nagarjuna wanted to show the futility of all views, both positive and negative, the ruthless nature of his method – one writer calls it a kind of philosophical sadism – has a tendency to nihilism. As a counter to this negative disposition there later arose a sub-school, the Svantantrika of Bhavaviveka and his colleagues, which took a more positive line.[6] An even more positive line was taken by the masters of the Yogacara or Vijñañavada school, who asserted the primacy of consciousness. The objects of the external world are not 'real' or external at all, they argued, but transformations of consciousness or mind. In support of this thesis they pointed to the fact that things can appear in the mind when there is no 'external' object present – in a dream, for instance, or through the practice of imaginative visualisation.

In other schools this is known as the teaching of Citta-matra or 'Mind Only'. In the West it is called Idealism, the notion that only minds and mental events exist, which opposes Materialism, the notion that only matter exists. The most distinguished proponent of Western Idealism is Bishop Berkeley (1685–1753), who maintained that to exist is to be perceived and that perceptions are just ideas in the mind. It might therefore be asked: if a tree, for instance, only exists while it is being perceived, what happens to it when there is no-one around to perceive it? Does it politely fade away? No, the worthy bishop would reply, it continues to exist even then – because all things are contained in the mind of God . . .

According to Buddhist hagiography, the seminal master of the school was a shadowy figure named Maitreyanatha. His more famous successors were two brothers, Vasubandhu and Asanga (both fourth century CE), who were natives of Gandhara. Asanga first studied with masters of the pre-Mahayana Mahishasaka school, but, after spending twelve years in meditative retreat and feeling that he had gained nothing, he became profoundly disillusioned. He then met a mangy dog, which inspired him with deep compassion. This was lucky, for the dog was the Coming Buddha, Maitreya, in disguise. Maitreya promptly initiated the kindly Asanga into the Mahayana and dictated many texts to him, including the *Yogacarabhumi* ('Ten Stages of the Yogi's Path').

Vasubandhu, meanwhile, had attached himself to the Sautrantika school, though he spent four years in Kashmir studying the Abhidharma system of the Vaibhashikas, a group of Sarvastivadin scholars. At first he was contemptuous of his brother's new-found wisdom, a system, he declared, 'so difficult and burdensome that it could only be carried by an elephant'! He was to rue those caustic words. Hearing some texts read, he was later so illuminated that he wanted to cut out his own tongue. He then read through one vast sutra in a mere fifteen days and nights, sitting in a bath of sesame oil to keep awake. Afterwards he became a great writer of Mahayana texts and commentaries himself, an expert debater, the founder of monasteries, nunneries, dharamsala (guest-houses) and hospitals, as well tutoring the son of the Emperor Govindagupta.

According to the Yogacara view, mind is subject to three levels of possible modification. There is citta, which includes the six kinds of sense consciousness; and there is manas, the 'I' consciousness. These develop from alaya-vijñana, the so-called 'store consciousness' level of mind, a kind of subconscious in which the experiences of the past are stored as 'seeds' (bija) of future experiences. This produces a momentary stream of consciousness whose waves subside when all the seeds are exhausted.

Yogacara was not just a speculative philosophical school. As its name suggests, it was based on yoga practice. So it was said of Vasubandhu that he was 'attempting to explain that which is beyond the power of words to convey, and which came to him by the mysterious way of profound meditation.' The philosophical aspect is therefore just upaya, skilful means, to point the devotee towards a profound insight that can only be gained through actual practice. This is the so-called 'revolution at the basis' (ashraya-paravrtti). When a person finally sees that external objects are just projections of his own consciousness, he realises that there is no object to be seized and no person to seize it. This leads to the Path of Insight which gives access to an ultimate state where, all the seeds of the alaya-vijñana having been exhausted, perfect quiescence in a deep samadhi of pure consciousness supervenes. This is devoid of all content, beyond the subject-object dualism, and as such is identical with the Dharmakaya. In the words of the master, Vasubandhu:

> When consciousness does not apprehend any object-of-consciousness, it is situated in 'consciousness-only',
> for with the non-being of an object apprehended, there is no apprehension of it.
> It is without citta, without apprehension, and it is supermundane knowledge;
> It is revolution at the basis, the ending of the two kinds of susceptibility to harm.
> It is the inconceivable, beneficial, constant ground, not liable to affliction,
> bliss, and the liberation-body called the dharma-body of the Sage.[7]

TATHAGATAGARBHA

The positive implication that the central mystery of man and the Universe enshrines a 'something' rather than a 'nothing' is also to be found in the Tathagatagarbha doctrine, which is expounded in texts like Ashvaghosa's *Awakening of Faith in the Mahayana*, the *Shurangama Sutra* and the *Tathagatagarbha Sutra*. This suggests that each person is a receptacle or womb containing the potentiality or embryo of buddhahood. It only needs right practice to remove the covering defilements and expose this eternal Reality.

This of course is to take Buddhism perilously close to an atman teaching, a fact not lost on some apologists, who asserted that the doctrine had only been taught as an upaya or skilful means for luring benighted Hindus, hopelessly addicted to the idea of atman, into the Buddhist fold. Later, of course, they would learn the error of their ways . . . Sophistry, surely?

HUA-YEN

The plethora of sacred texts that Buddhism produced was more than enough to perplex the ordinary mind. Understandably, then, attempts were made in mediaeval China to organise and classify the texts, indicating which the Buddha had prepared for those of high and which for those of lesser understanding. Schools arose accordingly. In each case, one particular text was claimed to be pre-eminent: the Summa of the Buddha's teaching.

The T'ien-t'ai (Japanese, Tendai) or White Lotus School was built around just such a project, its devotees venerating the *Saddharma-pundarika*. Another was the Hua-yen or Flower Adornment School, its devotees preferring the *Avatamsaka Sutra*, a vast compilation of texts, some undoubtedly originating in India, probably put together in Central Asia in the third or fourth centuries CE.

In the last book of the *Avatamsaka*, the *Gandavyuha*, we are told how a pious pilgrim named Sudhana is sent on a quest for Enlightenment by Mañjushri, how he traverses the ten stages of the Bodhisattva's Path and finally enters the tower of the Cosmic Buddha, Vairocana, under the guidance of Maitreya. Here he is presented with the stunning Hua-yen vision of the Universe: a universe as viewed through the eyes of an enlightened buddha sitting in the 'Samadhi of Oceanic Images':

> He saw the tower immensely vast and wide, hundreds of thousands of leagues wide, as measureless as the sky, as vast as all of space, adorned with countless attributes: countless canopies, banners, pennants, jewels, garlands of pearls and gems. . . . Also inside the tower he saw hundreds of thousands of other towers similarly arrayed; he saw those towers as infinitely vast as space, evenly arrayed in all directions, yet these towers were not mixed up with one another, being each mutually distinct, while appearing reflected in each and every object of all the other towers.[8]

Everything in the Universe, then, down to the humblest item, includes everything else, in totality – open a speck of dust and you will find an entire universe! – and yet, paradoxically, it does not in any way forego its own special distinctiveness. Thus, any one item is the 'cause' of the whole Universe, and, if it changes in even the most minute particular, the whole Universe changes too. Yet, in another and non-exclusive sense, that item is causally dependent on the totality.

So this is a grand panoramic vision of universal interdependence and interpenetration, hence popular among those with a 'green' or holistic cast of mind. It also cuts counter to the traditional Buddhist view of the world as an endless cycle of woes, for it positively affirms the world and all its constituents. Even the much castigated human being, the creator and slave of egoism, the cockpit of passion, can hold his head up again! As one writer has aptly put it: 'In the Hua-yen Universe, everything counts!'

ZEN

Such rarefied philosophies as we have been briefly discussing of course stand in stark contrast to the noble silence that the Buddha is said to have maintained when plied with questions of a metaphysical or speculative nature. However useful, they only amount to head knowledge; and it is in fact very easy to be immensely learned about Buddhism (or anything else for that matter) in a scholastic sort of way and be utterly unable to make the quantum leap to actualising the teachings – making them live in our own daily lives. To *know* all about Buddhism and to be a living example of it are in fact two very different things.

The Zen school arose in China in the sixth century CE precisely to grapple with this problem. There were in the monasteries and temples Buddhist monks and nuns who had accumulated a great deal of head-knowledge. They had also steeped themselves in Buddhist morality and the monastic code of discipline. But they were stuck and could not make the necessary quantum leap. What the early Zen masters provided, therefore, were powerful new methods – many of them iconoclastic by conventional Buddhist standards – for pushing those practitioners beyond thought and discipline, up to a whole new octave-level where they could directly see into the great mystery of things for themselves.

Generally, the Zen school looks positively at the great mystery at the heart of things. '*What is it?*' is one of the classic questions that practitioners are urged to address with unremitting energy. Yet the early masters would brook no answer that smacked however slightly of conceptual thought. They demanded one that was existentially authentic: that came directly from the heart, from the human centre that enshrines the great mystery of man and the Universe.

All Buddhist teaching, then, insofar as it bears upon that great mystery, is a kind of circumambulation around it. Different doctrinal approaches are formulated to suit the unique circumstances of specific times and situations. Yet in the end we must let go of all thought and verbiage, let go of everything in fact, so that the great mystery may live through us.

6 · MORALITY

In contemporary Western culture morals have become decidedly unfashionable. It just is not hip or sexy to keep to the rules and be good. This is largely because our own religious traditions have atrophied and their ethical bases degenerated into rigid codes inimical to change, development and healthy self-expression. On the other hand, living religious traditions, vitalised at source, produce dynamic and relevant morals, and in the past these have provided the springboards for great cultural advances.

We humans are essentially moral beings. Only in degenerate social conditions that stunt proper development do we become immoral. We *want* to be ethical. Indeed we *need* to be, for morals are the forms that mould the expression of our living energies, enabling them to manifest their highest potential: highest in terms of most beautiful, noble, creative and harmonious.

So as a first practical step on the Buddhist path, we put our lives in good order. Just doing this in itself makes us feel better, less ill at ease with ourselves and less at odds with the world at large. We become more peaceful, more trusting, and that in turn causes good things to happen back to us – and to those around us. A two-way process.

Ideally, ethics should spring naturally from the heart, but in the first instance, at the beginner's stage, most of us need some kind of code to guide us, though it is always more important to keep to the spirit rather than the letter. The basic code that Buddhism offers is Pancha Sila or Five Precepts. Monks and nuns observe many additional rules: the Vinaya Pitaka of the Pali Canon, which is today still observed by Theravadins, lists some 227 rules for monks. For the laity, however, initially at least, just five are deemed sufficient:

1: Killing

Firstly, there is the principle to refrain from killing any living being. This of course includes the almost universal injunction against the murder of other human beings; but it also extends to include all kinds of other beings as well – animals, birds, fish and insects – for they too are spiritual beings like us, possessing the potential for spiritual growth, which includes of course the possibility they might themselves sometime attain human rebirth. Animals may also be regressed humans, for according to the Law of Karma it is possible for humans who have behaved badly to be reborn in that state – or as denizens of the other lower realms.

To be true to this principle and not collude in murder after the event, many Buddhists become vegetarians, though this is not obligatory. Early Buddhist monks, for instance, being mendicants, could accept meat that was put into their begging-bowls. They were only required to reject it if they knew that its butchering had been done specifically for them. Some Mahayana schools were much more emphatic about vegetarianism, however. In the *Lankavatara Sutra*, for instance, the Buddha informs Mahamati:

> In the manner of the present sutra all [meat-eating] in any form, in any manner, and in any place, is unconditionally and once and for all, prohibited for all . . .[1]

Tantrists naturally have a different attitude. Meat actually figures as a sacrament in some rituals.

Altogether the matter of meat-eating remains a point of hot controversy in Buddhist circles. Some years ago I was at a meeting where HH the Dalai Lama was asked how he could eat meat. (Most Tibetans in fact do so; they could not have survived in the hostile conditions of the Roof of the World had they not.) He answered that there was no doubt at all that vegetarianism was the best policy. However, he had tried to be a vegetarian for two years but had suffered health problems. On the advice of his doctors, therefore, he had gone back to eating meat.

2: Theft and its Bed-fellows

The second principle is to refrain from taking that which is not given. That is, stealing and its variants – including 'liberating' articles from shops, 'borrowing' books and failing to return them, and all kinds of sharp practice, including many that have become socially acceptable in our go-getting society. In general, obtaining anything for oneself in ways that cause others to suffer is not morally sound, even if technically no law is breached.

3: Sex

The third principle is to refrain from irresponsible sexual activity: that is, activity that hurts others in any way.

As the strongest passion to which we are prone, sex is always highly-charged karmically. It can cause all sorts of things to happen, not least that a new life enters this world. It must therefore be regulated, but at the same time it cannot be safely repressed. As the thirteenth century Japanese Zen monk-poet Yoshida Kenko wrote:

> The passion of love is deep-rooted; its true source is a great mystery. There are desires connected with all the senses; all but this may be conquered. No-one is exempt; young and old, wise and foolish alike are its slaves. It is a terrible madness, one to be dreaded – yet one for which we should never reproach another.[2]

All sexual activity is of course proscribed for Buddhist monks and nuns, but it is understood that lay people will have sex lives – though, of course, this is not obligatory! Celibacy is quite a healthy state, if again it does not involve repression; that is, a denial or thwarting of the libido whereby it is thrust below consciousness.

On the matter of sex, however, one must say that generally Buddhism is not very positive. In the spectrum of religions it is way over on the ascetic, body-denying, monastic wing – the opposite, in fact, of Judaism and Islam, which seek to integrate sexuality into worldly and spiritual life. The Buddhist sutras and other works speak very disparagingly of this very natural instinct, basically because it was seen as the primary means whereby people become entrammelled in family life, which affords restricted opportunities for spiritual practice. When, for instance, the monk Sudinna lay with his former wife at his parents' request – they wanted grandchildren – the Buddha dressed him down soundly:

> Misguided man, [he said], it were better for you that your member should enter the mouth of a hideous, venomous viper or cobra than that it should enter a woman.[3]

And Shantideva (eighth century CE), author of the *Guide to the*

Bodhisattva's Way of Life, had to resort to strong aversion-therapy techniques to wean himself away from eros:

> If I am attached to what is unclean,
> Then why do I copulate with the lower parts of others' bodies
> Which are merely cages of bones tied together with muscles,
> Plastered over with the mud of flesh?
>
> I myself contain many unclean things
> Which I constantly have to experience;
> So why, because of an obsession for uncleanliness,
> Do I desire other bags of filth?[4]

Given these views, and assuming that the kind of sex envisaged by the Buddha and his followers was mainly of the basic marital sort with procreation as a primary motive, it is a question what these sages would have made of modern permissive sexuality, outside marriage, unconnected with procreation and concerned mainly with sensual pleasure and emotional satisfaction!

In general, then, the Buddhist message would seem to be: if you are serious about living the spiritual life, it is best to have transcended sex. The exception again of course is Tantra, which characteristically takes its stance at the opposite pole and seeks to integrate sexuality – indeed to use sexual energy as a means for gaining Enlightenment. Some modern Western Buddhists, such as Alan Watts, have also sought a similar integration, and understandably so, for as the psychologist C.G. Jung has pointed out, spirituality and sexuality have for too long been at odds, not just in Buddhism but generally, and a reconciliation is called for. Given that Buddhism is a non-dogmatic and dynamic religion which adapts to meet changing conditions, it may well be that this kind of reconcilation is something that will be attempted and achieved before too long – and probably in the West.

4: Speech

The penultimate principle is to refrain from harmful misues of the faculty of speech. These include lying, slander, malicious or idle gossip, misrepresentation, blackmail and so forth. Obviously these can cause pain to others and create disharmony – even Big Trouble. There is also another reason, and this relates to the importance of truth and its significance within spiritual life.

I once knew an inveterate and highly creative liar. He was indeed one of those people who make a principle of lying and only deviate from it when some really juicy inducement lures them to tell the truth. He was also very ambitious and in order to advance himself had concocted a quite amazing curriculum vitae. He was a doctor of this, a master of that – and he could also regale his listeners with wonderful stories of exotic places he had visited, relationships with famous people, miraculous experiences . . . all (or mostly – one never knew!) not true.

One day I was with him when he was being interviewed by a radio reporter, who asked, 'How old are you?'

My friend cocked his head and looked at the ceiling. 'I'm either twenty-eight,' he said uncertainly, 'or thirty-four . . .'

And I could see he quite genuinely did not know which was true. He had lied so much about his age that he had indeed lost track of precisely how old he was. Fantasy and reality had blurred into each other.

If we are really serious about living the spiritual life (or even a sane worldly life) we must keep a firm grip on truth, on *what is the case*, otherwise we may all too easily lose our bearings and fall victim to the many pit-falls with which the path is beset. We must most of all be clear about our own motivation – a kind of inner 'right speech'.

Sadly, in our culture truth is being debased all the time. We have politicians who lie and high officials who admit that they have been 'economical with the truth'. We have phenomena like 'creative accountancy' and, in public relations, we have elevated the manipulation of facts and figures and people's minds into a high (and highly rewarded) art.

5: Drink and Drugs

The final principle is to refrain from ingesting substances that befuddle consciousness. This includes alcoholic drink and the whole gamut of dope. Not only do these lead to heedless activity – many crimes, including crimes of violence, are committed under their influence – but they also impede awareness and, as we shall see in the next chapter on meditation, the development of awareness or clear-seeing is essential.

Drink and drugs are also often avenues of escape from the dark and difficult things of life, including our own problems. Indeed, problems cannot be effectively solved while a person is addicted to them. So there are many good reasons for not taking drink or drugs – or at least to the extent where they begin to impair awareness.

Of course, the monastic codes make drink and drugs absolutely off-limits for monks and nuns, but Tantra yet again has its own antinomian attitude to these things, and in lay circles in the West today things also differ from the patterns established in the East. In our cold, northerly lands, ale has traditionally been a staple beverage, spirits a comforter and wine a sacrament. Many Western Buddhists, therefore, (including the present writer) are not averse to a moderate amount of social drinking – moderate being the operative term here – though many others at the same time prefer to abstain completely.

Something must also be said about drugs. Since the 1960s, many genuine spiritual searchers have experimented with consciousness-raising drugs like LSD, cannabis, peyote and mescalin, and claim to have received profound experiences under their influence. Whether such experiences are really spiritual has been questioned; and in any case they do not produce lasting changes – only sustained practice can do that. There are also identifiable dangers connected with specific drugs, and the fact that they are illegal surrounds them with a paranoid ambience. However, no conclusive evidence for their spiritual relevance or irrelevance exists as little dispassionate research has as yet been done.

Right Livelihood

Additional to the moral precepts outlined above, in the Noble Eightfold Path, an early graduated scheme of the way to Enlightenment, we find mention of Right Livelihood. This means earning our living in ways that do not harm, deprive or exploit other people, animals and the environment. The modern obsession with economic growth has, however, produced a culture where anything goes as long as it makes money.

We can see that implicit in all five precepts is the age-old Indian principle of ahimsa: *not harming* – either others or oneself. We can safely extend this to the environment, the world as a whole and even to outer space. Nothing in fact falls outside the sphere of our moral responsibility. For instance, according the the Hua-yen school of Buddhist philosophy, which developed in mediaeval China, our every action affects the *whole* of the Universe.

The grave environmental problems we now face on Planet Earth stem directly from our ignorance of this fact. Yet, perplexingly, even as we begin to see what we are doing and what suffering it will bring down on both ourselves and our descendants, we find it very difficult to change our ways. Everyone is aware that it would be a good thing if there were fewer cars, but no-one wants to give up their own!

Of course, any harmful action will, according to the Law of Karma, refract back on the being that perpetrates it; and morally wholesome actions conversely induce positive come-back. But these Five Precepts should not be regarded as grave and rigid laws. The Buddha did not want to make us guilt-ridden or into rigid fundamentalists who grasp the letter of the law but miss the spirit. A lot of disharmony and suffering can be generated by stickling demands for strict adherence to principle, whereas a little good-hearted flexibility can make for more harmony and less complication. We see in the newspapers today, as in the past, how fanatical religionists are prepared to commit terrible crimes, like murder, to uphold some lesser principle.

The precepts, then, are in the nature of ideals or guidelines, to be used with flexibility and good sense. If we fail to live up to any of them, we should not torment ourselves with visions of hellish punishments. Rather we should learn from our failure and resolve to do better in future. Moral perfection is therefore something towards which we all-too-fallible humans aspire; it is not something we can hope to achieve totally and at once.

Nor should morality be used as a stick with which to beat others. If we have any degree of self-knowledge, we know a little about our own failings and so will not be too hasty in making judgements. The urge to judge in any case usually stems from projection of our own dark side. This causes us to see other people's failings glaringly well, for they are precisely the failings that we cannot bear to contemplate in ourselves! So the moderately wise person attends to his or her own faults, attempting to rectify them, and does not preoccupy him or herself overly with the faults of others.

Finally there is also this to bear in mind. The real aim of spiritual practice is not to serve the self-centred ego. Quite the opposite; it's about becoming free of the wiley ego's endless concern with self-interest. Now, most immorality is ego-serving and operates directly at the expense of others and the Universe in general. Morality is therefore a primary curb on the ego and a first step towards liberation from that whole nexus of compulsions.

7 · MEDITATION

What is meditation?

Remember Dr Johnson's pithy dictum: 'Depend upon it, Sir, when a man knows he is to be hanged, it concentrates his mind wonderfully.'

The truth is, we live our lives in a kind of waking dream. We are only hazily aware of what is really going on both outside and, even more so, inside ourselves. Every chance stimulus – every random meeting or event, every vagrant emotion, mood, impulse, – and so on – just sparks off a more or less automatic reaction. It needs a vital shock, like a stark confrontation with death, to jerk us awake. Then for a moment the scales of semi-sleep, subjectivity, projection and fantasy fall from our eyes and we see the world *as it really is*.

Meditation is about developing that kind of acute awareness all the time. And it means doing so without becoming attached to the objects of observation out of desire, or rejecting them from aversion. It means becoming the dispassionate watcher, the one who knows: becoming buddha, in fact. This is surely what the modern sage Jiddu Krishnamurti meant when he talked of 'choiceless awareness'. Buddhism traditionally has another word for it – Smrti (Pali, Sati): Mindfulness.

MINDFULNESS

The basic form of meditation that the early texts describe the Buddha as teaching is not sitting meditation, as one might have expected from modern formal practice, but something to be done by a monk as he 'fares along', going about his normal business. It consists of the specific applications of Mindfulness, described by the Buddha in the *Satipatthana Sutta*:

> There is this one way, monks, for the purification of beings, for the overcoming of sorrows and griefs, for the going down of sufferings and miseries, for realizing Nirvana; that is to say, the four applications of mindfulness. What are the four?
>
> A monk fares along contemplating the body in the body, ardent, clearly conscious of it, mindful of it so as to control covetousness and dejection in the world; he fares along contemplating the feelings in the feelings, the mind in the mind, and the mental objects in the mental objects, ardent, clearly conscious of them, mindful of them so as to control covetousness and dejection in the world . . .[1]

Although it is emphasised in this text that Mindfulness should be established 'precisely to the extent necessary just for knowledge, just for remembrance' and 'independently of and not grasping anything in the world', its application should be wide and deep and along prescribed lines. For instance, when in contemplation of the body, the practitioner should not be merely aware of his present posture or any action he may be performing; he should also at appropriate times reflect upon the nature of the body – the fact that it is like a skin bag containing various impurities, organs, bones, and so on. Special emphasis is laid on the gruesome aspects of the physical body, and if he passes a cemetery the practitioner is urged to reflect that his body too is of the same nature as those that now lie there 'swollen, discoloured, decomposing'. In this way, attachment to the body is undermined.

The benefits to be obtained from this practice are very high: 'either profound knowledge here-now, or, if there is any residuum remaining, the state of non-returning' (that is, the state of a being who rises to a higher world and reaches Nirvana without being reborn in this world again).

SHAMATHA AND VIPASHYANA

Later systematisers and the compilers of Buddhist meditation manuals subdivided meditation practice into two parts: Shamatha (Calm Abiding) and Vipashyana (Insight or Higher Vision). In the Pali language they are known as Samatha and Vipassana.

Shamatha is concerned with developing concentration – that is, the ability to maintain the focus of attention one-pointedly but without undue exertion on a chosen object – and with calming and stabilising the mind so that it is no longer disturbed by deluding excitations.

The establishment of these qualities of calmness and concentration are vital preliminaries for Vipashyana practice, which is the more active analysis and investigation of all phenomena that fall within the ambit of consciousness (these too are enumerated in some detail in the texts) with a view to a penetrative realisation of their true nature.

BASIC MEDITATION: HOW TO PRACTISE

Most practitioners sit on the floor on a small, plump cushion. They assume the classic cross-legged lotus or half-lotus position. If this is not possible, a straight-backed chair will do. The important thing is to keep the back straight (though not stiff or rigid) and the head balanced on the upright neck. The hands should be laid loosely in the lap, one lying inside the other or holding the other firmly. The eyes are then half closed and the arrow of attention turned inwards.

Now, letting go of all active preoccupations (planning, problem-solving, scheming, fantasising, and so on), we come fully into the here-now. Just allow yourself to relax alertly into the aware state. This state is not something we have to create. It is the ground of our being; all we have to do then is allow it gently to come into its own. So there should be no goal-oriented striving or forcing, only the exertion of sufficient energy to prevent us lapsing into an empty sleep-like or day-dreaming state.

Next, steer awareness towards a particular object. Uusually the rise and fall of the breath is recommended. Watch how it passes in and out of the nostrils, or watch the rise and fall of the diaphragm. Or you can concentrate on the 'fire-field' of the tanden or area some five centimetres below the navel – whatever is most comfortable.

Of course in the beginning – and indeed for a long time afterwards, for that matter – it is very difficult to keep awareness on target. The mind, accustomed for so long to its own wayward habits, will tend to wander away and be caught and excited by any thought that happens to stray into its ambit – and so off into the endless labyrinths of rumination. But now you can make a start at breaking this vicious cycle. Gradually you will experience moments when the mind is marvellously calm and clear, the heart at peace – but only temporarily . . . the old turmoil will relentlessly return, time and again. You must not be discouraged, however, or think you are a bad meditator. Meditation is one area where judgement or competition is right out of place. Instead just go back to the basic breath-watching practice and patiently persist with it. Also do not allow yourself to become attached to those wonderful moments of calmness and clarity, or contrive to reconstruct them. Attachment and striving will only inhibit their return. All you can do is go on, doing the best you can. There are in fact traditionally said to be five 'hindrances' which impede progress in meditation. They are sensual desire, ill-will (or aversion), laziness, restlessness and worry, and doubt.

Shamatha may release paranormal powers, known as *siddhis*. These classically include the ability to heal, to read people's characters (or minds) and foretell the future, to levitate and raise bodily temperature by many degrees at will, walk on water, multiply the body infinitely – and so forth. It is always emphasised, however, that these are by-products of spiritual practice, not objectives, and if they arise great care should be taken not to be seduced by them. The possession of powers can all too easily lead to ego inflation and the power-complex.

It is also possible to enter the dhyanas and samapattis, the so-called trance states and formless absorptions. These are eight increasingly rarefied states of mind in which sense perceptions and thoughts are progressively eliminated and consciousness becomes more and more subtle until merely the slightest residue remains. At the very apex of the system the practitioner may indeed enter a ninth absorption, Nirodha-samapatti (complete cessation of thought and consciousness), which is an experience of Nirvana-like bliss lasting for up to seven days.

Some practitioners practice Shamatha assiduously in order to enter the dhyanas and the samapattis, and the text-books recommend the use of special objects of concentration (kasina), such as coloured discs, for this purpose. But while all this may be interesting, it can also be another trap. Seduced by the bliss to be enjoyed in those subtle states, the practitioner can all too easily be stripped of all motivation to push on to the true end of the spiritual project, Enlightenment itself, which can only be attained through Vipashyana.

In Vipashyana or Insight Meditation, the calmness and concentrative ability forged in Shamatha are used to inquire penetratively into the true nature of things. Intense observation and analysis of phenomena encountered will, according to the classic texts, reveal that all are subject to duhkha, anitya and anatman; are inherently painful or unsatisfactory, impermanent and devoid of atman or self –

or put simply: 'everything that arises passes away and is not self.' This is not mere head-knowledge but a deep existential understanding that is at once purifying and liberating. More positively, it is said to also give access to the Unconditioned: to Nirvana.

Because most of us do not normally like to confront ourselves honestly, when we begin to open up the mind in meditation a great deal of repressed or forgotten material – what Jung would call aspects of our Shadow or Dark Side – will often rise into consciousness, sometimes disturbingly. If this happens, you should again observe that material, not getting caught up with it on one hand but certainly not trying to suppress or violently extirpate it on the other. For here you have a rare chance to undergo very effective psychotherapy. If you hospitably allow it, however dark or disturbing it may be, to enter consciousness and rest there, in full awareness, it will in time fade away quite naturally. Then you will learn the great truth that your biggest bogies – your deepest fears, guilts and pains; your most distressing problems – are no more substantial than the morning dew. Awareness, like the sun, will evaporate them.

MEDITATION ON LOVING-KINDNESS

Although the meditation techniques employed in Basic Buddhism, compared at least with those developed later, tend to be relatively simple and passive, there are some quite active forms. For instance, it is possible to use the so-called Brahma Viharas or 'Heavenly Abodes' as objects of concentration in Shamatha practice. The Viharas include loving-kindness (maitri), compassion (karuna), sympathetic joy (mudita) and equanimity (upeksha). The sending out of maitri to individuals in need – and in ever increasing circles, to the whole duhkha-torn world – is particularly favoured by modern Western practitioners.

This is a typical quotation from the sutras:

> There, O monks, the monk with a mind full of of loving-kindness pervading first one direction, then a second one, then a third one. then a fourth one, just so above, below and all around; and everywhere, identifying himself with all, he is pervading the whole world with mind full of loving-kindness, with mind wide, developed, unbounded, free from hate and ill-will.[2]

I was also once at a meditation session where the presiding monk suggested we direct loving-kindness to ourselves. He did this, he explained later, because so many Westerners do not like themselves very much – and if we do not like ourselves, how can we like yet alone love others?

Although this practice clearly embodies a concentrative element, it is also very much about generating particular kinds of thoughts and feelings, and so may fall a little outside what purists might regard as meditation. In other words, it has form, whereas 'true' meditation, it might be argued, is formless – or as near as possible. Yet within the early Buddhism schools – and indeed the later ones – texts on meditation enumerate long lists of worthy subjects upon which the calm and concentrated mind is encouraged to ponder deeply.

MAHAYANA BUDDHIST MEDITATION

Mahayana Buddhism, of course, has rather different objectives from those of the early schools. Rather than seeking nirodha, cessation, through the attainment of existential gut-knowledge of the truth of duhkha-anitya-anatman, the devotees of the Mahayana aspire to a similarly profound penetration of the truth of Shunyata, Emptiness, and make this a primary object of meditation. They also seek to generate bodhisattvic qualities so that they can work effectively in Samsara to alleviate the suffering of sentient beings. Yet for all that the meditation methods of most Mahayana schools rest firmly on a basis of Mindfulness and Shamatha-Vipashyana.

For instance, the early masters of the Yogacara school employed the Buddha's classic application of mindfulness method – again in a manner not restricted to the meditation cushion – though they made subtle adaptations to suit their own outlook and purposes. According to the great Vasubandhu, whereas the early Buddhists are mindful of merely their own bodies, etc., the bodhisattvas are mindful in two directions: both of their own and others' bodies, etc.; and they practise in this way, not merely to cultivate non-attachment, but 'neither for lack of attachment, nor for non-lack of attachment, but for a Nirvana which has no abode'.[3] Vasubandhu also felt that meditation should be preceded by preliminary practices of a more intellectual nature designed to give the practitioner insight into the mentally 'constructed' nature of the phenomenal world. Special antidotes should also be applied to the obstructing factors and positive qualities cultivated.

The seminal masters of the T'ien-t'ai school, which originated in China and whose devotees regard the *Lotus Sutra* as the Summa of the Buddha's teachings, also had their own distinctive views about Shamatha-Vipashyana. Chih-i (sixth century) maintained that Shamatha practice ('chih' in Chinese) could produce insight into Shunyata but of an imperfect, reclusive and passive sort. This could be corrected by Vipashyana practice ('kuan' in Chinese), which would, among other things, afford deeper insight into the true nature of things and generate practical bodhisattvic compassion. Taken together chih and kuan could bring about compassionate wisdom in which all phenomena could be seen as neither real nor unreal.

The T'ien-t'ai school was renowned for its meditation practices, which it classified according to a gradual, sudden and perfect paradigm. Four ways of attaining samadhi or one-pointed concentration were also delineated. These included meditation for ninety days on a proper subject (such as the Buddha); circumambulation of a statue of the compassionate buddha, Amitabha, for ninety days, and/or invocation his Holy Name; ninety days of sitting and walking practice aimed a rooting out defilements; and concentration upon Emptiness and the other characteristics of Ultimate Reality.

PURE LAND MEDITATION

On the face of it, the devotional Pure Land school might seem to have little to do with meditation. Its devotees take the view that, in the dark age in which we are living, we can hope to attain little by our own striving. All we can do is to throw ourselves on the mercy of the celestial buddha Amitabha. Where our 'self power' (Japanese, jiriki) is impotent, his 'other power' (Japanese, tariki) can save us by ensuring our rebirth in the Pure Land of Sukhavati.

Most of the Pure Land that has been transmitted to the West is of the Japanese variety, represented by the Jodo and the Jodo-shin schools, which place primary emphasis on the Nembutsu: the repetition of the name of Amitabha (Japanese, Amida). Such a practice must pacify thoughts and establish mental calmness, mindfulness and concentration.

Previously, in China, where Pure Land Buddhism came fully into its own, some of the early masters used more sophisticated methods of meditation, such as visualising Amitabha and his Pure Land and even formless kinds of meditation, which were thought to produce meditative states no less profound than those produced by the practices of other schools, such as the Zen school.

ZEN MEDITATION

The Zen school, known in China as Ch'an, might be called the meditation school par excellence. Ostensibly disparaging scriptural learning (though in fact squarely rooted in Yogacara and Prajña-paramita philosophy) and other practices (like performing rituals, reciting the scriptures, and so on), it emphasises direct seeing into one's own nature. The early Chinese Zen masters do not especially recommend sitting meditation; direct seeing can be accomplished – and sustained – in everyday life. However, later Chinese and Japanese Zen stress the importance of zazen or sitting meditation – and lots of it, both by day and at night. This, according to the Japanese master Dogen, is the 'front gate of the Buddha-dharma', and 'not just the practice of one or two buddhas; all buddhas and ancestors follow this way.' Hakuin, another Japanese master, meanwhile says that all other practices come back to sitting meditation, and that 'by the merits of a single sitting' the practitioner 'destroys innumerable accumulated sins'[4].

Legend has it that Zen originated in India, but really it came into its own in T'ang dynasty China. Of the so called 'Five Houses' that flourished then, only two have survived to the present, but these have been successfully transmitted to the West via Japan. They are the Lin-chi (Japanese, Rinzai) and the Ts'ao-tung (Japanese, Soto).

Soto Zen meditation (Shikan-taza) is usually practised facing a blank wall. The internal method – sticklers would no doubt call it a non-method – is essentially formless. Dogen, who transmitted the teachings of the school from China to Japan, declares that zazen is not learning to do concentration. It is not introspection. It is not thinking of good or bad. It is not a conscious endeavour of any kind. There should not be expectations. One should not even desire to become a buddha. Just –

> Sit solidly in meditation and think not-thinking. How do you think not-thinking? Nonthinking. This is the art of zazen.[5]

In this, practice and realisation are not separate. Just to sit is to be a buddha. 'The practice of beginner's mind is itself the entire realisation'. Dogen, who had seen as many as two thousands monks practising in this way both day and night in the great meditation halls of Sung dynasty Chinese monasteries, goes on:

> Therefore, I recommend to students ... to do zazen and endeavour in the way, depending on the teaching of the buddha ancestors, under the guidance of a teacher, without distinguishing between beginning or advanced, and without being concerned with ordinary or sacred.[6]

Meditation in the Rinzai tradition, on the other hand, is rather more militant. Practitioners sit in straight lines, facing each other. They begin perhaps with a Shamatha-type breath-watching or counting practice to bring about calmness and concentration. Then they traditionally apply themselves with concerted effort to koan practice.

Koan riddles (Chinese, kung-an) are generally based on the records of real life situations in which early masters enlightened their students. In Sung dynasty China, as Zen began to lose its original flair and vitality, these were collected in great anthologies like the *Blue Cliff Record* and the *Gateless Gate*. These formalised riddles, now having something of the significance of precedents in case law, are still handed out to Rinzai Zen practitioners today. Pondering them long and deeply, the student will attempt to give an 'answer' to the teacher, usually in Japan called a roshi or 'old master', in the course of regular interviews (sanzen). The roshi will then judge its authenticity. Any 'answer' that smacks however slightly of conceptualisation or phoney contrivance will be ruthlessly rejected. If, however, the devotee comes up with an acceptable answer, he or she may well be adjudged to have had a genuine breakthrough or satori. But that is just the beginning. More work must be done to deepen understanding. In other words, once a degree of calmness, clarity and concentration has been produced, the koan is an extremely active device for continually throwing the student against the ultimate question of his own nature.

A classic account of intensive koan practice is given by Hakuin, the revitaliser of Japanese Rinzai Zen. At the age of twenty-four, while staying at the Eigan temple, he grappled with the koan Mu ('No', 'Not') by day and night, forgetting both to eat and rest:

> Suddenly a great doubt manifested itself before me. It was as though I was frozen solid in the midst of a sheet of ice extending tens of thousands of miles ... To all intents and purposes I was out of my mind and the Mu alone remained ...

This state lasted for several days. Then I chanced to hear the sound of the temple bell and I was suddenly transformed . . . All my former doubts vanished as though ice had melted away. In a loud voice I called: 'Wonderful, wonderful. There is no cycle of birth and death through which one must pass. There is no Enlightenment to seek . . . ' My pride soard up like a majestic mountain . . . Smugly, I thought to myself: 'In the past 200 or 300 years no one could have accomplished such a marvellous breakthrough as this.'[7]

Unfortunately, his master dismissed all this as derived from study, not from the intuition.

'You poor hole-dwelling demon!' he jeered, much to Hakuin's chagrin.

Hakuin applied himself equally assidously to another koan – only to achieve the same humiliating result. Then one day he took his alms-bowl to a nearby town and was beaten by a madman. Strange to say, this produced enlightening results: he penetrated the meaning of various koans that had hitherto puzzled him. But again the Master neither approved nor denied what he said, though he stopped calling him a hole-dwelling demon. Hakuin then went back to attend his old teacher, Nyoka, who was sick. More breakthroughs followed, but it was not until he was thirty-two, at the dilapidated Shoin temple at Hara, that he at last perfected his understanding. Then he uttered a great cry and burst into tears, having come to the conclusion: 'Studying Zen under a teacher is not such a simple matter after all.'

Intensive Questioning: A Practical Exercise

The mind is first calmed and cleared. Positive as this is, it is not, as should be clear by now, the purpose of meditation. We have to go deeper, right down to the core of our being, and ask the ultimate question, 'What is this?'

Wield the question like a samurai sword. Cut down hard, striking for the core – 'What is this?' – again and again: 'What is this . . . ? What is this . . . ?'

Show no mercy – keep asking, keep looking down into the mystery of your inmost darkness. Don't look for a conceptual answer, or speculate; don't be deflected or defer the inquiry; look and ask now, this very instant: 'What is this . . . ? What is this . . . ?'

A Mandala

TANTRIC MEDITATION

Buddhist Tantra aims at bringing about Enlightenment very speedily by special yogic means. It is not, however, according to its own teachings, suited to everyone. Only special candidates who have already practised long and successfully gained deep insight into Shunyata (Emptiness) as well as having developed a high degree of bodhicitta qualify to practise it. Then they must forge a connection with a learned guru, who will initiate them into the mandala or sacred precinct of their chosen deity (yidam). The rite of initiation (abhisheka) that the guru bestows allows the devotee to perform a range of specialised rituals and practices (sadhana), many of which involve working with dark aspects of the psyche. Herein lie special dangers, so both to protect the unwary from burning themselves and the teachings from being debased Tantra is hedged around with a veil of secrecy, grave vows and other protections.

Buddhist Tantra possesses an extensive pantheon of yidam or deities. Some, like Avalokiteshvara, the Bodhisattva of Compassion, his female Tibetan form of Tara, and Mañjushri, the Bodhisattva of Wisdom, wielder of the adamantine sword that slices away all delusion, are benign. Others, like Yamantaka, Mahakala and Chakrasamvara, are wrathful (see page 85). All probably developed from ancient non-Buddhist Indian deities. Chakrasamvasa, for instance, is a Buddhist transformation of Shiva, the ascetic-erotic Hindu deity of death and regeneration.

Insofar as Tantra involves meditation it presupposes a solid basis in Mindfulness and Shamatha-Vipashyana (known in Tibetan as Shine-Lhatong). Given these, its own distinctive practices involve creative visualisation, which is carried out to a virtuoso degree of proficiency. The devotee will learn, for instance, to create the form of his chosen deity out of the bija or seed mantra that embodies the essence of the deity, the bija being firstly created out of the Emptiness of his own mind. The mental image of the deity must be built up in very precise detail and full colour according to archetypal patterns.

The Tantric yogi aims to eventually acquire the enlightened qualities of his yidam – which are really his own innate enlightened qualities. While this might be quite understandable in the case of benign deities, it is perhaps far less easy to understand in the case of wrathful ones, which in traditional iconography are depicted as extremely macabre beings with bloodshot eyes and flaring fangs, sporting necklaces of skulls, carrying skull-cups and daggers, and

A Wrathful Deity

surrounded by wreaths of fire. Some passionately couple with their shakti consorts – a symbol both of the union of wisdom and skilful means, and of the bliss of the Enlightenment which that union produces. For according to the Buddhist view such dark and passionate energies, when purified, also possess enlightened qualities.

At the apogee of Tibetan Buddhist Tantra lies Highest Yoga Tantra (Anuttara Yoga Tantra), which has two stages. The purpose of the first stage, the Generation Stage, is to practise transformation of the death, intermediate (or bardo) and birth states into the path. This prepares the Tantric yogi for the Completion Stage, where he will work with the subtle body. This consists of a number of centres (chakra) and channels (nadi), through which a 'wind-energy' (lung) circulates. In unreconstructed beings, because the channels are knotted up the circulation of the wind-energy is disrupted, resulting in our gross and deluded behaviour. The yogi, however, will consciously direct the wind-energy directly up through the chakras to the infinitesimal 'droplet' (bindu) in the heart chakra. This will purify and separate the subtle body from the gross body. Discursive thought is instantly expunged and the primordial enlightened state supervenes.

Clearly such practices are very different from the formless ones found in, for instance, Zen. However, there are formless practices in the Tibetan tradition, notably Mahamudra ('Great Seal') and Dzogchen ('Great Perfection'), though these are embedded in graduated systems that include formal practices.

According to 'The Song of Lodrö Thaye', a text of the Karma Kagyu school of Tibetan Buddhism:

> Since in the view of Mahamudra
> Analysis does not apply,
> Cast mind-made knowledge far away.
> Since in the meditation of Mahamudra
> There is no way of fixing on a thought,
> Abandon deliberate meditation.[8]

There is therefore nothing to acquire through Mahamudra; the practitioner is instantly one with the non-dualistic Dharmata or luminous ground of being. Dzogchen, which may have been subject to early Zen influences from China, is similar. Although traditionally a teaching of the Nyingma school of Tibetan Buddhism, it is taught in a trans-sectarian manner by Professor Namkhai Norbu, a master from East Tibet presently living in Italy. By Professor Norbu's account, Dzogchen is 'a teaching concerning the primordial state of being that is each person's own intrinsic nature from the very beginning.'[9] He calls this state 'Presence', and the serious practitioner strives to discover it in his own mind. Thereupon, abandoning 'distracted' living, he will remain centred in Presence amidst the hurly-burly of daily life.

FUTURE DEVELOPMENTS

At present most Western Buddhist meditators practise according to the time-honoured traditions of the particular Oriental school to which they feel drawn. There have, however, been fruitful experiments with combining traditional meditation methods and modern Western psychotherapeutic techniques. The latter are very good at dealing with blocks and problems frustrating development to the full ego stage – that is, the stage of mature autonomous individuality – while the Eastern methods serve very well in the 'transegoic' phases: the phases of consciousness beyond the 'I' stage.

A useful start has also been made, mainly in the USA, in the serious academic study of different traditional methods – in the jargon of the field they are known as 'consciousness disciplines' – and the psychospiritual world of consciousness in which they operate.

Finally, it is to be hoped that, as mediators become increasingly proficient, there will be a new phase of experimentation and innovation, perhaps with combinations of meditation techniques from different schools and traditions. This arguably more than anything else would be warranty of the continuing vitality of Buddhist meditation.

8 · THE PRINCIPAL SCHOOLS AND TRADITIONS

1. THERAVADA BUDDHISM

Tracing its roots back to the seminal Sthaviravada school that arose in India after the Buddha's death, the devotees of the Theravada or 'Way of the Elders' would argue that their tradition is the true repository of the teachings and practices propagated by Shakyamuni himself. In their eyes it therefore stands as a fixed pole of orthodoxy and tradition amidst the mêlée of 2,500 years of change and development. Others would, however, dispute this, arguing that the Theravada is itself a very much later development and that consequently it can make no claims to special priority.

Whatever the truth of the matter, the Theravada survives today as a living tradition in Sri Lanka, Burma and Thailand, and it is from these countries that it has been transmitted to the West. The Pali Canon is still very much its scriptural foundation, and the Pali language rather than Sanskrit is used for chanting and other liturgical purposes. A lively tradition of Pali scholarship exists, also an active tradition of meditation. In the East, while the scholar-monks tend to gravitate to the larger temples and monasteries where facilities exist for their work, the dedicated meditators are more likely to seek out secluded places. These 'forests monks' may live in outlying monasteries or else alone in caves or huts like the early Sangha (Community). Some wander from place to place, accepting whatever in the way of food or shelter may be offered to them – or not offered. This is regarded as a form of dhutanga or hard practice, and is considered to be particularly beneficial for shaking off the defilements.

As a sign of their renunciation of worldly values, monks and nuns shave off all their facial and cranial hair, and wear the traditional ochre or orange robe. Having committed themselves to a life of poverty and mendicancy, they have few possessions, but one essential is a bowl into which lay devotees may put food. They also vow themselves to chastity, and the most scrupulous will neither carry nor touch money. All strive hard not to be idle or to fritter energy away in self-indulgences, like unnecessary sleep or gratuitous chatter. Bounded as they are at all times by their numerous precepts and rules, they have in any case to be constantly mindful of what they are doing and able to accept a very high degree of circumscription. Hierarchy is important too. When addressing those senior to them – that is, those who were ordained earlier than they were – monks should bow and generally show due respect.

At the British Theravadin monastery that I visit, the monks get up very early – at 4.00 am – and go to the shrine-room, where they chant for some time before the great gilded image of the Buddha, then sit in silent meditation. According to the rules, they are only allowed to eat between dawn and noon. They therefore have a simple breakfast of plain rice gruel and tea. Afterwards chores are done, and some monks will leave on the daily alms round (Pali, pindapad), taking their begging bowls with them. As food donated by the laity is prepared in the monastery kitchen by lay-brothers (anagarika) and laity, this Oriental tradition might be thought unnecessary. However, it is maintained out of respect for tradition and also so that the community can keep in touch with the local people. The substantial meal of the day is duly taken before 12.00 noon, then there is a period of rest before the afternoon work-session begins. Tea is taken in the late afternoon, plus certain allowable 'medicines' like cheese or black chocolate. Then at 7.30 pm it is back to the shrine room for more chanting and silent meditation. At about 9.00 pm monks and nuns are free to go to bed, but must be ready to rise again when the bell rings at 4.00 am.

This austere daily routine goes on year in, year out, punctuated only by periods of retreat when the community draws together for more intensive practice. Some monks or nuns may also embark on solitary retreats, or go off on dhutanga – the 'hard practice' mentioned above, when they wander from place to place, usually in the West accompanied by a lay-brother or a layman. There may also be visits to schools, local Buddhist societies and other places to deliver discourses (Pali, desana) and/or lead meditation.

Within this particular community, any person wishing to take the robe has first to serve a probationary period of at least one year as an anagarika. He (or she) then shaves both head and face, dons a white robe and lives by eight precepts – that is, the Five Precepts (see chapter 6) plus three additional ones: not to eat at wrong times; to refrain from dancing, singing, music, attending shows, wearing garlands and using perfumes and cosmetics; and not to lie on a high or luxurious bed. In addition he or she will be encouraged to take on board some seventy-five rules of etiquette.

His term as an anagarika completed, a man may request to be given the monk's precepts – 227 of them in all, though only about twenty are of practical significance today – at a ceremony held before the annual Vassa or Rains Retreat in a sima or consecrated space. He will then be able to wear the ochre (or orange) robe. A woman, on the other hand, cannot become a fully-fledged nun (Pali, bhikkhuni) as the order of nuns has technically died out, but she may take the vows of a Dasa Sila Mata or Ten Precept Sister, which is what we mean by 'nun' in the present context. This is done at a ceremony in the shrine-room when she will exchange the white robe for a brown one. She is then bound by the eight precepts listed above, of which the seventh, concerning dancing, singing, and so on, is divided in two, plus an additional precept prohibiting the handling of money, gold and silver. She will also take on numerous training rules. Four rules, known in Pali as Parajika Offences, are considered especially grave and anyone transgressing them would be expelled from the order and not allowed to rejoin. These concern sexual intercourse, deliberate killing, deliberate stealing and claiming to possess paranormal powers. All the rules are rehearsed by the whole community twice monthly on Uposatha days.

A life circumscribed by so many rules, which drastically curtail personal liberty and self-expression, might seem a very bleak prospect. Many who have actually lived it, however, report that after initial struggles they actually begin to feel more free – free in particular from the burden of self and its endless conflicts and demands. This leads at times to the welling up of great joy and a sense of serenity. Of course, if the life does not prove suitable, a monk or nun may leave at any time by handing their robes back to their preceptor, though as this is regarded as a serious step they will be counselled first and asked to pause before making a final decision.

Leaving does not, however, debar anyone from seeking reordination later.

The traditional relationship between Theravadin monastics and laity is one of useful symbiosis. The monastery is the spiritual focus of the locality in which it is situated. Monks live and practise there, and the laity may come to stay for a period of retreat or just for a brief visit. Uposatha days – full and half moon days – and festivals draw large crowds of lay devotees, who come with dana (gifts), including food to offer to the monks and nuns. Afterwards there may be a communal meal and there is usually much conviviality. There will be a certain amount of ritual too: chanting from the Pali scriptures is usual, the delivery of a blessing, a discourse from the abbot, perhaps a period of silent reflection, and the recitation of the Five Precepts. The Three Refuges may also be taken when, led by the monastics, the laity will chant the Pali formula:

> Buddham saranam gacchami;
> Dhammam saranam gaccham;
> Sangham saranam gacchami;

– repeated twice more with the prefix 'dvutiampi' first and then 'tatiampi'. Taking refuge in this way is an important rite, affirming or reaffirming one's faith in Buddha, Dharma and Sangha. It is thus a kind of Buddhist confirmation. It is also open to different levels of interpretation: for instance, on one level one may be affirming one's faith in the historical Buddha, Shakyamuni, but on another one may be affirming faith or confidence in one's own Buddha-nature: the buddha within.

Special ceremonies are also carried out at monasteries to celebrate rites of passage – birth, marriage and death.

The principal Theravada festivals include the celebration of the Buddha's Birth, Enlightenment and Parinirvana – called Wesak in the Sri Lankan tradition, Vaisakha Puja in the Thai – on the full moon day of May; and Kathina in October or November, which celebrates the ending of the three-months Rains Retreat when monks withdraw into their monastery for intensive practice. At Kathina the laity bring special gifts for the Sangha, notably cloth for robes.

There is a school of thought that maintains that real practice is possible only if one ordains into the Sangha. However, in recent years there have been successful attempts in the West to establish intensive lay practice on the basis of a particular meditation technique. Especially influential have been the Burmese 'noting' and 'sweeping' systems pioneered by Mahasi Sayadaw and U Ba Khin, and

successfully propagated to Westerners by Joseph Goldstein, Sharon Salzbu
S.N. Goenka and others.

2. TIBETAN BUDDHISM

The Tantric Buddhism of Tibet could not stand in stronger contrast
to the Theravada. When travellers familiar only with the Southern
School first encountered it they thought that if indeed it was
Buddhism then it could only represent a fall from the high spiritual
standards set by the Buddha.

To walk into a Tibetan temple is to be confronted by raw primary
colours – red, blue, green, mustard – the mingled aromas of strong
incense and butter lamps, the benign and wrathful deities depicted
on scroll paintings hanging on the walls or painted on the walls
themselves, and a rich array of gilded figures and votive objects.
If there are lamas present, one may hear the monotonous, guttural
drone of their chanting, periodically augmented perhaps by the
cacophonous clash of cymbals and the wailing of thigh-bone trumpets
and other instruments. Here are suggestions of magic and mystery
which resonate with something suppressed and half-forgotten in the
depths of our being. Small wonder, then, that Tibetan Buddhism is
probably the most popular form of Buddhism in the West today,
barring the fast-growing Nichiren cult.

Their seclusion on the Roof of the World enabled the Tibetans to
preserve the Mahayana and Tantric Buddhism of India for over a
millennium and to create a uniquely rich spiritual culture. Unfortunately in 1950 the Chinese Communists felt the need to 'liberate'
these people from the thrall of Western imperialism. Despite the
fact that there were virtually no Westerners – and certainly no
imperialists – in Tibet at the time, the Chinese went ahead. . . and
became imperialists themselves, taking over the government of what
had hitherto effectively been an autonomous nation, colonising it,
plundering its mineral and natural wealth, and making the Tibetans
themselves virtual aliens in their own land. The Tibetans voted with
their feet against this 'liberation', and when the Chinese finally – and
bloodily – completed their takeover in 1959, tens of thousands fled
to exile in India. The virtual destruction of Buddhism in Tibet was
completed during the Cultural Revolution (1966–76).

Yet these violent and destructive events did have one positive
outcome: they made the spiritual riches of Tibetan Buddhism accessible to Westerners for the first time. After 1959, lamas – including HH

the Dalai Lama – began to visit the West and Tibetan Buddhist centres were set up, the first being Samyé Ling, established in the lowlands of Scotland in 1967 by two Karma Kagyu lamas, Akong Rinpoche and Trungpa Rinpoche. Others followed, and today we can claim that four major schools are well-established on Western soil:

The Nyingma School

The Nyingmapa[1], or followers of the tradition dating back to the first transmission of Buddhism to Tibet, tend to be rather more anarchic than the Sarmapa ('New Ones'), less inclined to monasticism and decidedly more inclined to magic. They particularly venerate the Tantric adept Padmasambhava (Guru Rinpoche), who originally came from Oddiyana in what is now the Swat Valley of Pakistan. Having overcome the occult forces inimical to it, he successfully transmitted Buddhism to Tibet in the seventh century CE. This great siddha did not apparently deliver all his teachings at that time, however, but cunningly hid some – the so-called termas or 'treasures' – in both geographically-locatable places as well as 'in mind', so that they could be discovered later when people would be better qualified to understand the deep wisdom they contained. The general Nyingma classification of teachings tends to be slightly different from that of the other schools and it opts for a six-fold rather than a four-fold classification of Tantras. The last head of the school, HH Dudjom Rinpoche, a married lama, died in France in 1987.

The Sakya School

There was a time during the twelfth and thirteenth centuries when the high lamas of the Sakya school, which takes its name from its great monastic headquarters in southern Tibet, were vassal kings of Tibet under Mongol overlordship. Before its fortunes fell into decline, the school also enjoyed great spiritual influence. Its most important doctrinal and meditational cycle is *The Path and its Fruit*, a systematisation of both Sutra (that is; pre-Tantric) and Tantric teachings credited to the ninth century Indian adept Virupa and based on the *Hevajra Tantra*. This has both an exoteric and an esoteric presentation. According to Ngakpa Jampa Thaye (David Stott):

> The philosophical viewpoint which informs *The Path and its Fruit* is the notion of the inseparability of Samsara and Nirvana. . . It is said: 'By abandoning Samsara one will realize Nirvana.' Mind itself, the union of Luminosity and Emptiness,

is the root of Samsara and Nirvana. When obscured it takes the form of Samsara and when freed of obscurations it is Nirvana. The key to Buddhahood, the ultimate source of benefit for all beings, lies in this realisation.[2]

By following this path one can apparently attain Enlightenment in a single life.

The Sakya school has now two sub-sects, the Ngor and the Tshar. Its present supreme head is HH Sakya Trizin, who was born in Tibet in 1945 but is based in northern India.

The Kagyu School

Practical mysticism rather than bookish scholarship characterises the Kagyu school – 'Kagyu' literally meaning 'Transmitted Command'.

Hagiography tells us that one of its seminal Indian masters, Naropa (1016–1100 CE), devoted a great part of his early life to scholarship, eventually attaining high office at the great monastic university of Nalanda. A vision of an old crone then revealed to him the hard truth that the knowledge he had acquired was merely dry intellectual stuff, not the trans-rational knowledge of the heart. The effect was traumatic; it drove Naropa to the verge of suicide. He was saved, however, by the discovery of his own guru, Tilopa (988–1069 CE), who had himself received instruction from the primordial buddha Vajradhara. Over a twelve-year period, Tilopa put Naropa through a gruelling course of Tantric training.

After the suppression of the first transmission of Buddhism to Tibet by the evil king Langdarma, a generation of Tibetans collected gold and departed to India to obtain teachings and texts. These were the lotsawa ('translators'). One of them, Marpa (b. 1012), travelled three times and studied with Naropa as well other great masters. Among the teachings he received were the so-called Six Yogas of Naropa and Mahamudra. The Six Yogas include Tumo, which, as a side effect, generates such a degree of physical heat that wet towels placed on a yogi's body in icy conditions will dry out quickly. Mahamudra ('Great Seal'), meanwhile, is a very high practice giving direct access to the luminous Dharmata or ground of being.

On returning to Tibet, Marpa settled down to an ordinary life as a farmer and family man. His most famous disciple and heir to the Kagyu lineage was Milarepa (1052–1135), who, because he had foolishly dabbled in black magic, had also to be put through an extremely rigorous course of training. Never ordaining as a monk and avoiding institutions, Milarepa became the much-loved prototype of the freewheeling yogi who pursues his own spontaneous spiritual path in lonely places. He gained many wonderful powers as a result of his austerities and was able on one occasion to defeat a priest of the Bön religion in a contest of magic for the possession of Mount Kailas, the great sacred mountain in Western Tibet. He was a poet too.

Milarepa's most influential disciple was the 'Doctor of Takpo', Gampopa (1079–1153), author of the classic text, *The Jewel Ornament of Liberation*. From his disciples stem three Kagyu sub-schools, the Drug, Drigung and Karma. The last head of the Karma Kagyupas, the Sixteenth Gyalwa Karmapa, died in Chicago in 1981, but not before seeing his school successfully transmitted to the West. The credit for this is due in large measure to the work of Chögyam Trungpa Rinpoche (born 1939), who, having fled Tibet and received a Western education at Oxford, helped set up a Kagyu centre in Scotland before moving to the USA, where he founded the extensive Vajradhatu organisation with headquarters in Boulder, Colorado. Gifted with unique talents as a Dharma teacher, plus a fair salting of fleshly frailties, controversy – even notoriety – dogged Trungpa for much of his short-lived teaching career.

The Gelug School

As its name – Gelug means 'Virtuous' – suggests, this began as a reform movement initiated by Tsongkhapa (1357–1419; also known as Jé Rinpoche), a pious monk from north-eastern Tibet. Wishing to see Tibetan Buddhism restored to the pristine purity of its Indian sources, Tsongkhapa attacked what he believed to be heretical views, notably those of the Jonang school, whose followers had reputedly adopted a form of soul or atman doctrine. He also stressed the importance of a basis of ethics and, for monks, the monastic virtues (strict celibacy, abstention from intoxicants and so forth), and he encouraged study so that practitioners might obtain a clear intellectual understanding of the nature and aim of the Buddhist path. He felt particularly strongly that a firm grounding in the Sutra teachings should be obtained before any attempt was made to negotiate the heady world of Tantra.

In his *Lam Rim Chenmo* ('Great Exposition of the Graduated Path [to Liberation]'), Tsongkhapa outlines preliminary practices relevant to the Sutra level of training. These include development of faith in the guru or teacher and correct motivation; meditation on impermanence and the preciousness of human birth, on karma and sufferings of beings in the six destinations of existence; and practices aimed at the accumulation of merit and the elimination of 'black karma'. The practitioner is urged to investigate and test the teachings at every stage, as a goldsmith assays gold, in order to ascertain, through reasoning, whether they are truly valid. In his *Ngag Rim Chenmo* ('Great Exposition of the Mantra Path'), meanwhile, Tsongkhapa deals with Tantra, which, as in all Tibetan schools, is the apogee of spiritual practice.

Gelugpas wishing to follow the path of philosophical study to the highest levels follow a special programme of higher studies. A monk completing this and passing his monastic examinations will be awarded the title of geshe. One Westerner has to date been awarded a geshe degree, but many others have ordained as monks and nuns and trained in Gelug monastic centres in both the East and the West. The time-honoured system of debate is still practised in both the Tibetan and English languages; also reflective meditation on the stages of the Graduated Path and the visualisation techniques of the Tantric system. Many of these Gelug centres are directed by Tibetan monk-lamas and, although the aim is to preserve the purity of the tradition, many spiritual directors nowadays incorporate elements of Western culture, such as psychological approaches. The needs of lay people, who may practise to as high a level as they are able within the constraints of their everyday lives, are also catered for at many of these centres.

Tsongkhapa's chief disciples founded the Gelug school, which enjoyed both spiritual and temporal preeminence in Tibet from the sixteenth century down to 1959. It was the Mongols, the original patrons of the school, who bestowed the title 'Dalai Lama' on its third head, 'Dalai' meaning 'Ocean (of Wisdom)', and also retroactively on his predecessors back to Gendun-drup, putative nephew and disciple of Tsongkhapa. The present incumbent, the fourteenth, is the monk Tenzin Gyatso, born in 1935 in eastern Tibet but presently living in Dharamsala, his 'capital-in-exile' in the foothills of the Indian Himalaya. The Fourteenth Dalai Lama's great spiritual qualities, his warmth and cheerfulness, and the way in which he has led his people through one of the most difficult periods of their history, always advocating a non-violent response to Chinese violations in Tibet, won him the Nobel Peace Prize in 1989. He is, along with the Fifth and the Thirteenth, one of the great Dalai Lamas.

The Lama in Tibetan Buddhism

It is hard to overestimate the importance of the lama in the Tibetan tradition. The word means a guru or teacher, who may be either married or a celibate monk, though not all monks (gelong) teach. The commentary to Tsongkhapa's *Foundations of All Excellence* explains that 'the very root to Enlightenment is the practice of reliance on a spiritual teacher.' It goes on:

> Having realized that the spiritual teacher is the root of all excellence, by continuous effort of body, speech and mind, develop great faith that recognises his knowledge and does not observe in him the slightest fault. Remember his vast kindness with deep gratitude, and honour him; make offerings to him, respect him in body and speech, and strive to put his teachings into practice.[3]

Whilst most teachers live impeccably and practise what they preach, some are unfortunately discovered to have feet of clay. Asked about this, HH the Dalai Lama told an audience in London in 1985:

> It is said that it is important for a student, prior to making a Dharmic connection with someone as a teacher, to understand what the qualifications of a guru or lama are in accordance with what is set forth in the Vinaya (that's to say, the Discipline), what's set forth in the Discourses [Sutras] and what's set forth in Tantra. Then it's also said that a person who wishes to become a teacher must understand what these qualifications are and work at fulfilling them.
>
> Then in the Mantra [Tantric] system there is a mode of procedure for highly-realised adepts whereby they engage in activities that are not usually allowed. Effectively, this is when they have achieved stability. What is meant by stability? It is when the adept has the capacity to actually overcome in others the loss or lack of faith that such activities might usually cause. . . However, if a lama does not have this capacity and we think, 'Oh, these are the grand activities of a high lama,' then we are in a difficult situation and must make up our minds as to how to proceed.[4]

3. ZEN

The legendary origins of Zen go right back to the Buddha. Because of the limited understanding of the majority of his followers, the story goes, Shakyamuni was forced to teach in words and concepts. There were higher teachings, however: non-verbal ones involving the direct transmission of understanding from the heart of the teacher to that of the disciple, completely by-passing the head. Such a teaching took place when Shakyamuni simply held up a flower, the monk Kashyapa got the message and an exchange of knowing smiles signified a profound spiritual transaction had taken place.

The school is said to have been transmitted to China in the sixth century CE by an Indian monk named Bodhidharma. He was presented to Emperor Wu of Liang, who asked about the meaning of the Buddha's teachings. 'Great emptiness; nothing at all holy,' Bodhidharma replied, implying that endowing temples and performing other pious works would not lead to realisation, only to the accumulation of good karma. The Emperor then asked, 'Who is facing me?', to which Bodhidharma replied, 'I don't know.' Leaving the Emperor nonplussed, Bodhidharma then departed and spent many years meditating before a blank wall at the Shaolin temple, a place still famous for its martial arts connections. Later he reluctantly began to teach.

Legends aside, Zen – Ch'an in Chinese – is really a Chinese development, incorporating elements of the indigenous traditions, notably Taoism. It properly came into its own with the sixth Patriarch, Hui-neng (638–713 CE), an illiterate who was suddenly enlightened on hearing the *Diamond Sutra* recited while selling firewood. He then went to study at the temple of the Fifth Patriarch, Hung-jen (601–74), and was put to work on the threshing floor. When Hung-jen wished to appoint his successor, he invited his students to show the depth of their understanding by submitting poems. All the monks deferred to the head monk, Shen-hsiu (c. 600–706), who reluctantly pinned up a poem in which he compared the mind to a bright mirror from which the dust (of thought) had constantly to be wiped. The next night the 'barbarian' from the threshing floor submitted a second poem in which he pointed out that, since the Buddha-nature is always clear and bright, 'where is there room for dust?' This proved to Hung-jen that Hui-neng did indeed possess a deeper understanding of Zen that Shen-hsiu, but he dared not openly confer the transmission on him as he knew it would infuriate the other monks. He therefore gave him the patriarchal robe privately and told him to leave – quickly.

According to tradition, the rivalry between Hui-neng and Shen-hsiu split Ch'an into two schools. The Southern School of Hui-neng favoured the notion of sudden Enlightenment, while the

Northern School of Shen-hsiu favoured the gradual variety. Further sub-divisions occurred and subsequently Five Houses and Seven Schools emerged, all basically propagating the teachings of the Southern School. Of these only two survive today, the Lin-chi and the Ts'ao-tung, which were successfully transmitted to Japan. Zen was also transmitted to Korea, where it is known as Son, and to Vietnam, where it combined with Pure Land in a successful local synthesis.

Classic Chinese Zen (Ch'an)

Very little Chinese Zen remains today. In any case, the golden age of the school was over a millennium ago, during the T'ang dynasty (618–907 CE). Afterwards it became formalised and lost much of its original vitality, though it survived – and indeed more successfully than the other schools – and still occasionally produced an outstanding master, such as Hsü-yün, who, when he died in 1959, was reputed to be 120 years old.

But what was the vintage Ch'an of the T'ang dynasty like?

After centuries of immersion in the teachings brought from India, Chinese Buddhists at last felt confident to make their own unique approach to the core of the Buddha's spiritual project. It was clear that intellectual study could only produce dry head-knowledge, not the direct trans-rational 'un-knowledge' of the heart. So the early masters laid primary emphasis upon *direct seeing* into the self nature and improvised ingenious ploys to achieve this – shouts and clouts, bizarre behaviour and repartee:

> One day as the master [Pai-chang] was walking along with Ma-tsu [his teacher], they saw a flock of wild ducks fly by. The ancestor said, 'What is that?' The master said, 'Wild ducks.' Ma-tsu said, 'Where have they gone?' The master said, 'Flown away.' Ma-tsu then grabbed the master's nose; feeling pain, the master let out a cry. The ancestor said, 'Still you say, "Flown away"?' At these words the master had insight.[5]

This is Enlightenment, not at some indefinite time in the future, but right here, now, without any shilly-shallying. For in Ch'an the highest realisation is not to be postponed until we are completely purified or have gathered a plethora of scriptural knowledge or clocked up a record-breaking score of meditation hours. To strive for goodness or knowledge, even to seek Enlightenment or to become a buddha, is indeed to pile up further obstructions to attainment. It is like running all over the world looking for a pearl that is fixed to one's forehead.

As Huang-po told an audience, quoting sutra: 'What is called supreme perfect wisdom implies that there is really nothing whatsoever to be attained.'[6]

If this is so, how then is one to practise? According to Pai-chang, like this:

> When things happen, make no response: keep your minds from dwelling on anything whatsoever: keep them for ever still as the void and utterly pure (without stain): and thereby spontaneously attain deliverance.[7]

And Huang-po:

> I advise you to remain uniformly quiescent and above all activity. Do not deceive yourselves with conceptual thinking, and do not look anywhere for the truth, for all that is needed is to refrain from allowing conceptual thought to arise.[8]

The field of Zen, therefore, is mind – our own minds; for the One Mind or Buddha Mind and our own minds are not essentially different. According to Pai-chang, 'The nature of mind has no defilement; it is basically perfect and complete in itself.' Our problem is that we sully it with our greed and desire; with discriminative thoughts of good and bad, like and dislike, existence and non-existence; with our concern with past and future – but most of all with our attachments. If we let it all go, mind returns to its native purity, free of obstructions like a shining mirror that can reflect whatever passes into its ambit because it is empty. Precisely this is buddhahood. But it is not to be confused with blank tranquillity. That is yet another trap. Ch'an Enlightenment leans neither towards activity nor to quietude. The mind should abide nowhere and in nothing – not even in not-abiding!

Classic T'ang dynasty Ch'an did not emphasise formal sitting meditation (tso ch'an; Japanese, zazen) as an end in itself. Rather, sitting stilled both mind and body and thereby created the 'inner potentiality' for direct insights to arise in everyday life. Furthermore, many now take the view that the differences between the various sub-schools were not particularly marked.

Japanese Soto Zen

T'sao-tung Ch'an was transmitted from China to Japan by Eihei Dogen (1200–53), where it became known as Soto Zen. It was transmitted to him by Ju-ching, the abbot of T'ien-t'ung Mountain, a stickler for monastic discipline and single-minded intense sitting meditation (Japanese, Shikan-taza). Ju-ching was the one truly impressive Ch'an master that Dogen came across during his spiritual wanderings in 'Great Sung' (China).

Dogen had become a monk at the unusually early age of 13, the deaths of his aristocratic parents having forcefully impressed the truth of impermanence upon him. Later he developed a 'great doubt' while studying at the famous centre of the Tendai school on Mount Hiei. In the *Mahaparinirvana Sutra* it was stated that 'all beings everywhere have the Buddha-nature'; but if this is so, Dogen pondered, why do we bother to practise at all? This set him off in search of an authentic teacher.

Dogen attained a Great Enlightenment during the summer retreat of 1225, when Ju-ching shouted, 'When you study under a master, you must drop the body and the mind; what is the use of single-minded intense sleeping?' Two years later he returned to Japan 'empty handed' – that is, not bearing scriptures or relics but being himself a living exemplar of the Buddha's teaching. He spent the rest of his life teaching, firstly in Kyoto and later away from metropolitan temptations and pressures in a remote and comfortless province, where he established the temple of Eihei-ji. Having been advised by Ju-ching to live in steep mountains and dark valleys, avoiding cities and villages, and not to approach rulers or ministers, Dogen likewise urged his own followers to drop the pursuit of wealth and fame, those perennial hindrances to the spiritual life, and instead to dedicate themselves wholeheartedly to practice. He was a fairly prodigious writer too, his great work being *Shobogenzo* ('Treasury of the True Dharma Eye'). He died in Kyoto, where he had gone seeking medical help for an illness.

Central to Dogen's teaching is the importance of intensive sitting meditation and the notion that we are not potentially but *actually* buddhas when we sit. Practice and realisation are one and immediate. Implicit in this is rejection of the notion that in the current dark age realisation is impossible. He also evolved some original ideas of his own, notably that the Buddha-nature is not beyond impermanence, it *is* impermanence. And, finally, though he taught both monks and laity, men and women, he believed very strongly in a sound monastic basis and worked hard to create that.

Japanese Rinzai Zen

Lin-chi Ch'an was transmitted to Japan, where it became known as Rinzai Zen, by Myoan Eisai (1141–1215). Like Dogen, who came after him, when Eisai returned from China he ran into trouble with the powerful Tendai sect, which succeeded in getting the Zen sect prohibited by imperial edict. Unlike Dogen, however, Eisai was prepared to compromise, and both Tendai esotericism and Zen meditation were practised alongside each other in his temples. Though he was in no doubt that Rinzai Zen represented the quintessence of the Buddha's Dharma, Eisai felt its hour had not yet come in Japan. Nevertheless, he laid a foundation upon which subsequent Japanese and Chinese masters could build.

Early Japanese Rinzai masters tended to go to Kyoto, the imperial capital, and Chinese masters to Kamakura, where the Shogunate or Military Governorship was established in 1185. This was the real centre of power, for the rising samurai class had by now eclipsed the old imperial aristocracy. The samurai found Rinzai Zen very much to their liking, and a dynamic 'on-the-instant' warrior Zen evolved in Kamakura, which used, not the classical formalised koan riddles, but ones improvised on the spot using an incident or situation with which the trainee was familiar. What, for instance, might a samurai do if, while getting naked into his bath, he found himself surrounded by a hundred armed enemies? Would he beg for mercy or die fighting? How might he manage to win without surrendering or fighting?

After the initial vitality of the Kamakura period, Japanese Buddhism went into a long decline. Because it enjoyed the favour of the Shogunate, the Rinzai Zen sect survived most successfully of all the schools, and during the fourteenth and fifteenth centuries lavishly endowed temples flourished, notably the so-called Five Mountains in Kyoto, which are extensive complexes adorned with the finest works of art. Such places fostered that high aesthetic refinement we associate with the Zen arts. But overall the drift both then and thereafter was towards institutionalisation, formalisation and state regulation, and down to modern times there was little in the way of significant innovation or development, except in the lives and works of two masters, Bankei and Hakuin:

Bankei Yotaku (1622–93) was one of those rare spirits who have the courage to find their own unique spiritual path, even if it means bucking against some of the hallowed conventions. His teaching sparkles with originality, and it was certainly highly effective in his own day, for huge crowds drawn from many different persuasions came to hear his discourses. At a time when Zen had become an élite preserve requiring command of classical Chinese and other recherché talents, Bankei was able to transmit its essence to ordinary people in terms they found accessible. He also had a gift for inspiring his listeners with confidence in their own spiritual potentiality. He even addressed 'mere women', telling them that they possessed the Buddha Mind just as men did.

Born into a samurai family, Bankei was something of a tearaway as a child; but then, in one of the Confucian classics, he discovered a reference to something called 'Bright Virtue'. This fascinated him to the point of obsession and he wandered far and wide in search of someone who could explain the meaning of the term to him. Unfortunately, the teachers he met were not of very high calibre, so he had to look for an answer within himself. Many years of intense, even desperate endeavour ensued and eventually his health began to crack. Then one day he flushed a gobbet of clotted phlegm from his throat and felt strangely refreshed. In the same instant he realised that – 'Everything is perfectly managed with the Unborn, and because up till today I couldn't see this I've been uselessly knocking myself out!'[9]

This Unborn is, of course, the same 'Unborn, Not-become, Not-made, Not-compounded' that the sutras mention. It is also the pure, shining mind of the Zen masters. But unlike most other masters, Bankei came to the conclusion that it is not necessary to go through protracted rigours and austerities to discover it. Nor does he seem to have thought very highly of formal practice: he talks disparagingly of 'device Zen' which depends upon techniques. The monks in his monasteries did meditate – presumably they had to do something! – but he did not lay heavy obligations or rules on them. The important thing is to discover the Unborn, and this can be done simply and directly, even by lay people. The trick is then to remain with it amidst the hurly-burly of everyday life. If thoughts arise, they should neither be suppressed nor indulged, for to be caught by them is to exchange the Unborn Buddha Mind for that of a fighting demon, a hungry ghost or some other tormented victim of bad karma. One should just remain detached and see that thoughts are transient illusions with no real substance. They will surely pass, leaving only the shining Unborn Buddha Mind – and in the marvellous, effortless functioning of this one can have complete confidence.

Hakuin Zenji (1686–1769) was a completely contrasting character who never lost faith in the rigours and austerities of hard practice and underwent them fully himself. Small wonder then that he spoke critically of Bankei's laid-back approach, and also of other sects and schools where practice fell short of his own unremitting standards. Quiestists, syncretists and Pure Landers came in strongly for his strictures. For him, the quest for Enlightenment was an heroic life-and-death venture to which one should commit everything. There was, however, a less severe, aesthetic side to his nature that expressed itself through the Zen arts of calligraphy, painting and poetry. He was also concerned with propagating Buddhism among ordinary people, and in this context he was prepared to relax a little and make a few concessions to human frailty.

Hakuin is now generally regarded as the revitaliser and reformer of the Rinzai system of training, and his influence, unlike that of Bankei, has been a lasting one. In particular he revised and extended the koan system, organising it into a strict programme of formal study. To 'pass' one koan is not enough. After every 'breakthrough' one must forge ahead to new thresholds. Three requirements are necessary in order to be able to meet the challenge: great faith, great doubt and great perseverence. Great doubt, or 'raising the great ball of doubt', an extreme state of spiritual intensity, is particularly emphasised. It is like 'a pair of wings that advances you along the way':

> When a person faces the great doubt, before him there is in all directions only a vast and empty land without birth and without death, like a huge plain of ice extending ten thousand miles. . . Within his heart there is not the slightest thought or emotion, only the single word Mu [lit. 'No' or 'Not']. It is just as though he were standing in complete emptiness.[10]

We have already observed Hakuin's own intense struggles with the koan Mu, but the fact is that the stress of them made him seriously ill. Luckily he was able to cure himself of this 'Zen sickness' by rerouting the vital energy (Sanskrit, prana; Chinese, chi) to the area below the navel (tanden). The precise method is outlined in his texts, Orategama and Yosenkanna. This touches upon an alchemical aspect of Zen that goes right back to its roots in China and derives from Taoism. It presumes that spiritual practice collects vital energy and uses it to break through to Enlightenment.

Korean Zen (Son)

The characteristics of Korean Zen are rather different from those of the Japanese variety. It is both less martial and formal, and a little more earthy. There is also strong emphasis on the Vinaya, and both the bhikshu and bhikshuni orders have survived. Nuns have their own nunneries, and their status is not materially lower than that of the monks. Generally, Son preserves something of the flavour of classic Ch'an, and, in a limited way, has been transmitted to the modern West.

When the Rinzai tradition was first brought into Korea from China, it met with local resistance. This did not stifle it but it did force it to embrace elements of other traditions. A syncretistic Zen consequently emerged in the form of the Chogye order, founded by Chinul (1158–1210). Between the thirteenth and the mid-twentieth centuries, Buddhism was eclipsed by Confucianism, but the Chogye order emerged again in 1945, at the end of the long Japanese occupation, on an upsurge of nationalistic feeling.

Korean monastic practice incorporates three main elements: study, meditation (Son) and chanting (a Pure Land element). There are separate halls for each of these activities in the monasteries, and monks or nuns are free to specialise in whichever they find most conducive. Study focuses mainly on the Zen records and Mahayana sutras, chanting on the repetition of the names of the Buddha and the Bodhisattvas, and meditation on sitting and koan or hwadu practice. Usually a monk or nun will work on one hwadu, a koan-like question, throughout their training, most probably the ultimate riddle: 'What is it?' Monks and nuns come together for two three-month meditation retreats in the winter and summer seasons.

Western Zen

For most of this century there has been a two-way traffic of Westerners going to Japan to study Zen and Japanese teachers coming to the West. The result is that both the Japanese Rinzai and Soto traditions have been transmitted here and numerous centres established.

The emphasis in Western centres has mainly been on promoting lay practice, though in some the forms of Japanese monasticism, or quasi-monasticism with married 'monks' and 'nuns', have been established. Everywhere, however, the centre of activity is the zendo or meditation hall, which is usually a model of Japanese-style order and simplicity, with a shrine at the far end and neat rows of zafus or meditation cushions facing each other across an empty central aisle. It is here that regular sittings take place, and periods of intensive retreat known as sesshin. Following tradition, Soto students sit facing the wall and engage in their 'just sitting' practice, while Rinzai students face each other and, if so instructed by their teacher, engage in koan study. From time to time an official may march around the room, carrying a stick known as a keisaku. Those meditators who are becoming drowsy or losing muscle-tone may ask to be struck smartly on the shoulder muscles with this. There is likely to be chanting too, the rhythm beaten out on a mokugyo or 'wooden fish'; also much bowing and impersonal formality. Everything is regulated by strict rules, and this lends the atmosphere an edge of severity and purposefulness.

Because of the traditions of direct transmission and lineage, the Zen master or teacher – who may bear the title roshi ('old master') – continues to be of central importance in Western Zen. Students should have regular interviews with him (or her) and during the course of these a fairly intense relationship may be built up. Ideally a teacher should be able to read how students are progressing, note their blockages and guide-push them forwards. A sizeable amount of power is, of course, invested in this role – its origins go back to feudal models – and unfortunately this has been abused by some less than impeccable teachers, resulting in quite serious crises at a few Western centres.

4. PURE LAND

Shakyamuni Buddha is said to have saved himself 'by his own efforts alone', and this streak of spiritual self-help runs right through Buddhism. You will still hear people today saying that, 'You have to do it for yourself – no-one else can do it for you,' which is correct, but not altogether true. For faith and devotion perennially arise within the human heart, faith signifying belief that an external agency can help the individual spiritually, and devotion a deep gratitude for the source of that help. There have been such elements in Buddhism from the earliest times. To practise within the Buddhist tradition is in fact to display faith (though hopefully not blind faith) in that tradition. To bow before an image of a buddha or bodhisattva, a teacher or a monk or nun is to show both faith and devotion. So is to light incense, to copy or recite the scriptures, to carve images, to endow temples and monasteries, to feed the Sangha, and so on. Such tendencies grew as the religion itself developed, particularly during its Mahayana phase.

An important early devotional practice was that of Buddhanusmrti or 'Recollection of the Buddha'. This is done by bringing the Buddha to mind, reciting his name, and by visualising his image and/or his Pure Land or field of activity, which might be either a physical or a transcendental 'place' depending upon the sophistication of the individual view. It is also possible to go beyond recollection of the Buddha as a physical being to a more formless kind of recollection. The benefits to be derived from such practices are considerable. One might have a vision of the Buddha, or attain profound meditative states.

With the rise of the Mahayana we find the emergence of a number of cults of divine buddhas and bodhisattvas, such as Avalalokiteshvara, Mañjushri, Maitreya and Kshitigarbha. Each has his (or her) own Pure Land. Those drawn to these cults will recollect and worship these divinities in various ways, and pray for them to intercede spiritually on their behalf.

Chinese Pure Land – Ching T'u

Though the devotional strand in Buddhism was just one strand alongside others, a separate tendency did establish itself and a distinct school eventually emerged. This was the Pure Land school, which grew out of the cult of Amitabha, the Buddha of Infinite Light.

Though Pure Land historians produced the obligatory line of patriarchs going right back to the Buddha and including such Indian luminaries as Vasubandhu and Nagarjuna, the school undoubtedly reached its full flowering in China. It is based on the legend, recorded in the *Larger Sukhavati-vyuha Sutra*, of an ultra-bodhisattvic monk named Dharmakara, later to become the buddha Amitayus ('Infinite Life' – an aspect of Amitabha – see page 108), who vowed to create a Pure Land of peerless splendour and not accept Supreme Enlightenment until all sentient beings so wishing had been reborn there. The pious dead would emerge from lotus buds into this Pure Land, the Western Paradise of Sukhavati, where all defilements would be rapidly expunged and Nirvana attained in just one more lifetime.

This legend inspired pious Chinese Pure Landers to be in the best frame of mind at the moment of death in order to proceed smoothly to Sukhavati. Many chose their hour of death in advance, took a

Amitabha Buddha

bath, lit incense and sat upright to await the end, well secluded from grieving relations who might upset their state of mind. But was this Sukhavati a 'real place', a heaven with tangible features and adornments, or a metaphor for Enlightenment itself? This would again depend upon the sophistication of the individual view.

Also important to Pure Land is the old Buddhist myth of the 'Last Days of the Dharma' (Japanese, Mappo), which maintains that, after an initial period of vitality, the Buddha-dharma will enter a declining phase and finally a long dark age will set in when conditions will be so inimical that it will be impossible to achieve anything by one's own spiritual efforts alone. All one can do is throw oneself upon the mercy of a benign buddha like Amitayus-Amitabha, whose compassionate Other Power (Japanese, tariki) can achieve what cannot be done by the exercise of Own Power (Japanese, jiriki). Sixth century China, with its despotic governments, Buddhist persecutions, degenerate priests and prevailing desolation, seemed a perfect image of this predicted dark age, and the Pure Land cult consequently became very popular.

Three early Chinese patriarchs are of especial importance: T'an-luan (476–542), Tao-ch'o (562–645) and Shan-tao (613–681).

T'an-luan delineated five practices: 1. To make prostrations to Amitabha and wish to be reborn in his Pure Land; 2. To sing the praises of Amitabha and recite his name (in the formula, Namu O-mi-to-fo – 'Prostrations to Amitabha'); 3. To vow to be reborn in his Pure Land; 4. To visualise Amitabha and his Pure Land; and 5. To transfer merit to other living beings. He also believed that the name of Amitabha encapsulated all that this buddha stands for, so, like the dharani or magical phrases of the early Buddhists, the recitation of Name in the formula O-mi-to-fo ('Prostrations to Amitabha Buddha', known as the Nien-fo) possessed spiritual power that could ensure the practitioner rebirth in the Pure Land.

Tao-ch'o, who argued that the recitation of Amitabha's name is a particularly suitable practice for the present dark age, transmitted the Pure Land teachings to Sh'an-tao, who 'systematised Pure Land thought and brought it to its highest peak of development in China'.[11] He is also the author of the parable of the Two Rivers and the White Path:

A Pure Land Everyman, travelling westwards, finds his way contracted to a thin white path running between two rivers: one of water and one of fire. Behind, robbers and wild beasts are baying at his heels. With almost certain death at all sides, what can he do but forge ahead? He is encouraged by a man calling from the opposite bank, who promises that if he does so with 'single-heartedness and true thought' he will be protected. He walks on – and duly reaches the western shore safely.

This allegorically depicts the Pure Land view of man's place in the world. It is a horrendously dangerous predicament. The only hope is to seek salvation in the Western Paradise of Amitabha. The moment a practitioner decides to do this with complete faith, help comes from the 'other side'.

Throughout its history Buddhism has tended to be the preserve of the members of an intellectual, spiritual and social élite, and the focus has almost everywhere been in the monasteries. Pure Land Buddhism, however, has more general appeal. It offers an 'easy practice' that can be implemented in the world, without becoming a monk or nun; and it promises salvation to everyone through Amitabha's vows – to those still entrammelled in the passions, even to those who have committed serious crimes. Profound study and meditation are moreover distrusted as they are seen as leading to intellectual and spiritual arrogance.

Pure Land was therefore the first really democratic form of Buddhism, stressing humility rather than attainment, and as such became hugely successful among ordinary Chinese. Pious societies were spawned under its auspices, like the White Lotus Society, which developed into a sizeable property-owning movement before eventually being suppressed. In its heyday, the good works of its devotees included providing public amenities (bath-houses, hostels, mills, etc.), donating cloth, copying sutras and hosting vegetarian banquets. It was unusual in having married clergy and allowing women to play a prominent part in its affairs. Of the various schools that burgeoned in T'ang dynasty China, only Pure Land and Ch'an (Zen) had the vitality to survive the great persecution of 845. Indeed, in China the methods of both schools were often practised in tandem for double effectiveness – 'like a tiger wearing horns.'

Little Chinese Pure Land has been transmitted to Europe, but it is well represented in North America. It was first introduced there in the late-nineteenth century by the thousands of Chinese immigrants coming to work in the California Gold Rush and on the Union Pacific Railroad.

THE PRINCIPAL SCHOOLS AND TRADITIONS

Japanese Pure Land

Once transmitted to Japan, Pure Land became concentrated and simplified: the remaining vestiges of Self Power, including residues of 'hard practice', were stripped away, and primary importance placed upon the Nembutsu (the recitation of the name of Amitabha, known in Japan as Amida, in the formula Namu Amida Butsu), and ultimately on pure faith and grace. Again, its propagation was helped by the fact that the grim Pure Land world-view of Mappo resonated with the social realities of Japanese life at the end of the Heian Era and the beginning of the Kamakura. Civil strife, famine, disease, rapine, social breakdown and other evils made ordinary people very receptive to the notion that they were living in degenerate times and so were in need of some special method (or non-method) of salvation.

Two figures are of particular importance in Japanese Pure Land: Honen Shonin (1133–1212), founder of the Jodo-shu ('Pure Land School'), and his disciple, Shinran Shonin (1173–1262), founder of the Jodo Shin-shu ('True Pure Land School').

As a Tendai monk, Honen was sincere and dedicated, but he gradually became convinced that he lived in a fallen age and despaired of making any spiritual progress, even by pursuing the Amidist practices applied within the Tendai school. Only the 'easy practice' of the Nembutsu possessed any efficacy, he felt. Even one utterance was sufficient to ensure salvation, though continuous recitation was a healthy discipline, keeping the mind centred on the ultimate goal. In 1175 Honen left the Tendai school and began to teach according to his own convictions. A highly respected and effective monk, he attracted large followings, but this provoked the jealousy of other sects, who eventually managed to get his movement suppressed. In 1207 Honen, along with several disciples, was exiled to a distant province. He was allowed to return to the capital in 1211, a year before his death.

Honen is not regarded as an innovator. He did not advance Pure Land teaching any further than Shan-tao; but he did lay the foundation for an independent Pure Land movement in Japan.

Shinran too served an early spiritual apprenticeship as a Tendai monk, and his efforts again merely led to frustration and conflict. He came to feel that he was an utterly hopeless case: ridden with lust and ego, vain, greedy, sinful. . . Tainted in fact by all the vices, he was incapable even of performing a simply decent act let alone of saving himself spiritually. Later, he met Honen and the Pure Land

111

teachings and, since he was convinced that he was damned in any case, decided that he had nothing to lose by embracing them. He was banished along with Honen in 1207, and married in exile – he eventually fathered six children – thereby precipitating himself into a limbo of 'neither priest nor layman'. Afterwards, fully adopting the Mahayana view that Samsara is Nirvana, he rejected the dichotomy of lay life and monastic life, and propounded the view that the passions, far from needing to be expunged, are necessary to salvation. In 1211, he was pardoned along with Honen and later went with his family to preach in the Kanto area, where he attracted a considerable following. He receded into rather active retirement in Kyoto in 1235, continuing to teach, study and write. In 1262, lying on his right hand side, 'his head toward the north and his face to the west', he died with the name of the Amida on his lips.

Shinran probed deeper than Honen and came to the conclusion that the actual recitation of the Nembutsu is not as important as the underlying quality of faith, which he equated with the Buddha-nature itself. Faith cannot, however, be contrived by an effort of will – an effort of Self Power. It is pure grace: a gift bestowed by Amida, whom Shinran regarded as the ultimate Buddha and, in his formless aspect, one with the pure Dharmakaya. The Nembutsu itself bubbles forth as a natural expression of gratitude once faith is given. Concomitant with faith is a sense of the utter futility of Own Power, but this does not lead to self-rejection. On the contrary, it allows one to accept oneself totally, vices and all, for one is saved in spite of them.

There is a tendency in the West for Pure Land Buddhism to be down-graded as a low-level spiritual path: a kind of Buddho-Christianity for simple souls incapable of shaping up to the demands of, say, Zen or Tantric practice. This is a misrepresentation. Stripping away the theology and mythology, what Pure Land is saying is that we must let go of all self-initiated activity, have complete faith in the Buddha-nature within and allow it to function in its own mysterious way without interference from the thinking mind. In this way it is not very different from Zen – or other forms of Buddhism. The Nembutsu concentrates and clears the mind, and focuses on the Buddha-nature within.

The Pure Land schools of Honen and Shinran survive to this day, and have been highly successful at the popular level in Japan. They still eschew monasticism and all the frills and excrescences of religious life, concentrating on a simple theology of faith and Nembutsu practice that can be applied in everyday life. Japanese Pure Land Buddhism has also been transmitted to Europe and

North America, but has not been particularly successful, though championed by important pioneer Buddhist writers such as D. T. Suzuki and Alan Watts. Suzuki thought that Shin Buddhism might well one day prove to be Asia's greatest gift in the West, while Watts, tracing cross-connections with Jung's psychology, was very drawn to the Shin teaching of self-acceptance and the notion that we are saved as we are, warts and all. Such notions contain inherent problems, however, for if we are saved as we are, why bother to improve ourselves spiritually or attempt to lead moral lives?

5. NICHIREN

There is much talk nowadays of Buddhism as 'the fastest growing religion in the West'. Ironically, the brand of Buddhism attracting the largest number of new followers is regarded by many as the least representatively Buddhist of all the schools. This is the Nichiren Sho-shu or 'True Nichiren School', the most successful of the various sub-schools that trace their roots back to Kamakura Era Japan and a Tendai monk named Nichiren Shonin (1222–82). Today, Nichiren Sho-shu propagates an attractive form of 'Designer Buddhism' with an uncomplicated central chanting practice that draws pop and soap opera stars, fashion and media operators – and hordes of mainly young people.

Nichiren himself was a product of the same fraught milieu as Honen and Shinran. Like them, he became convinced that he was living in the degenerate age of Mappo, but, having been ordained into the Tendai school, he became convinced that the *Lotus Sutra* embodies the true teachings of Shakyamuni Buddha and that complete faith in it is the sole key to salvation. Other Buddhist schools, he came to believe, did not merely disseminate futile teachings and practices; they were downright pernicious insofar as they diverted people from the One True Path. Not that one had to deeply study and reflect upon the *Lotus Sutra*, however. The text's title encapsulated the totality of truth in the universe and as such was an embodiment of Shakyamuni Buddha. As a practice, therefore, Nichiren prescribed the Daimoku or chanting of the formula Namu-myoho-renge-kyo – 'Homage to the Lotus Sutra of the True Law'.

Nichiren started to proselytise in 1253 – and from the start there was a strong political dimension to his work. He not only unrelentingly denounced the other schools – he regarded this as a religious practice in itself – but called upon the authorities to suppress them. All the natural and social calamities of the time stemmed from failure to embrace the *Lotus Sutra* and toleration of heterodox schools, he declared. And in 1268, when a Mongol invasion threatened, he warned that only faith in the *Lotus* could save Japan. Such aggressive outspokenness naturally alienated the other schools, who in their turn called upon the authorities to suppress Nichiren. He was physically attacked several times and exiled twice. An attempt was also made to execute him, but this miscarried and merely served to vindicate his own sense of righteousness. In fact, all efforts to suppress him merely fired up his own sense of divine mission. He was eventually pardoned and, having lived for a time in a secluded mountain retreat, died at Ikegami.

Schisms arose within the Nichiren school after the founder's death, one cause of controversy being relations with other schools. Some groupings favoured a more moderate approach, while others advocated the hard line of 'neither to receive nor to give' (fujufuse). Nichiren Sho-shu is definitely of the latter, tracing its spiritual roots back to a thirteenth century hard-liner named Nikko, although actually founded in 1937 by a pragmatic educator named Tsunesaburo Makiguchi (1871–1944). As a movement with the alternative title of Soka Gakkai ('Value Creating Society') it burgeoned along with other 'new religions' after the military defeat of 1945, when the Japanese suffered a grave collective trauma. Its first leader during the post-War period was Josei Toda (1900–58), who promoted it so successfully (if controversially) that by 1960 it could claim the loyalty of 750,000 households. Toda was succeeded by Daisaku Ikeda (b. 1928), who, judging from the movement's newsletters, spends much time discussing peace with world political leaders. Ikeda founded a political party, the Komeito ('Clean Government Party'), though this has since had to sever its connections with Soka Gakkai.

Nichiren Sho-shu teaches that our destiny lies in our own hands. We must take responsibility for our own lives and make the necessary positive moves to settle our problems and realise our full potential. To these ends, members are actively counselled, helped and supported by the movement, and are encouraged to take up a three-fold practice involving faith, study and chanting. Faith is faith in the power of the Gohonzon, a scroll on which Namu-myoho-renge-kyo is written in mandalic form. The original, penned by Nichiren himself, is lodged in the head temple of Taiseki-ji at the foot of Mount Fuji, but members obtain their own copy and perform Gongyo before it twice daily. Gongyo involves chanting Namu-myoho-renge-kyo, plus selected passages from the *Lotus Sutra*. Finally, there is study of the

Buddhist teachings as reformulated by Nichiren and his successors. All this can be carried out without renouncing the world. Indeed, wordly success is valued within Nichiren Sho-shu, though it is also taught that it cannot lead to lasting happiness. That is only possible by sublimating the lower energies to higher purposes.

Currently, Nichiren Sho-shu is unique in avoiding relations with other Buddhist groups. It still affirms that Nichiren's teachings, which it describes as 'revolutionary' and hence difficult for many other Buddhists to accept, are uniquely suitable for our time. Furthermore, Nichiren himself was, as we have seen, never loath to stir up controversy and hot emotions. He thought them creative forces. Following the founder, therefore, Nichiren Sho-shu maintains the old tradition of shakubuku or vigorous (some might say aggressive) proselytising.

Other Nichiren sub-schools that have been brought to the West, albeit less successfully than Nichiren Sho-shu, include Reiyukai and its off-shoot Rissho Koseikai; also the Nipponzan Myohoji order founded by Nichidatsu Fujii (1885–1985), a man deeply influenced by Mahatma Gandhi. His white-robed monks and nuns have built peace pagodas in many parts of the world, and otherwise work tirelessly and harmoniously with other groups to promote world peace.

9 · THE WESTERN BUDDHIST SPIRITUAL QUEST

The spiritual search to find out who we really are is the greatest adventure. It is the quest for the Holy Grail, for the pearl of great price, for the crock of gold at the rainbow's end. True, ordinary lives are full of all kinds of seeking and striving. Yet the lesser goals that we set up – wealth, power, love, fame, and so on – are really false goals: diversions from what should rightly be our main purpose. At heart we know this, yet time and again we shy away from the challenge, daunted by what it demands of us and what we fear we may have to give up. All the frenzied business of our frantic world, therefore, is really so much running away from our true purpose.

It is an irony that, on the one hand, human ingenuity has probed the depths of space, and, on the other, the minutiae of the atomic world, yet we know least about that to which we live closest: ourselves. Of course there have been people throughout history who have explored this area, and they have left us guide-books and maps. But not so many. We can follow them, but not exactly, for life is an ever-changing labyrinth and we have to find our own routes to its centre. So we are on the leading edge of evolution. Stripped of their superficial personal trappings, our problems are the problems of the Universe – which is not a fixed or preordained Universe, but an experimental one – as it struggles to find its way forward out of the impasse of the present. No others have travelled into the future ahead of us. We are the frontiersmen and women.

We usually have to be driven out of our complacency to embark on the spiritual quest. A devastating crisis, much suffering, or a growing tiredness of going round and round, repeating the same increasingly meaningless patterns: these are the common precipitating factors. It was certainly so in my own case, when I left a comfortable conventional life in England and set out for India in 1971. Then one had to go to the East if one wanted to find wisdom and teaching. Today it is quite different. There is probably a Buddhist group in your own town, and a centre within a morning's car drive. For during the last twenty years there has been a kind of explosion of Buddhist developments here in the West. Temples, monasteries and centres have sprung up like mushrooms, with the result that one can now probably find better and more accessible teaching in the West than in the East, which is anyway now moving rapidly in the direction of materialistic acquisitiveness. Recently a Korean professor visiting the centre where I live remarked with a sigh, 'Now one must come to the West to find Oriental calm!'

The main problem that besets the modern newcomer, therefore, is not difficulty in obtaining teachings but the embarrassment of too much choice. At which counters of the spiritual supermarket to shop? Which of the tempting brands to choose?

Really, though, we are in a very fortunate position. Because all of the major Buddhist schools and traditions have now been transmitted to the West, we have a clearer view of what is on offer than our former Asiatic co-religionists. We can therefore allow ourselves a period of shopping around, experimenting with this and that in order to find out what suits us best. Of course, there are some people who just go on shopping around for ever, leaving a particular counter whenever difficulties arise and never really confronting themselves or the demands of Buddhism. So at some point one usually has to make a commitment to a particular course of study and practice, but it is best not to hurry the process. Commitment will generally arise quite naturally of its own accord when a situation feels right, whereas forcing the issue can lead to trouble. Many teachers and groups are moreover eager to recruit and will sometimes subtly (and sometimes not so subtly!) pressure a newcomer to join their party. On the other hand, many newcomers eagerly desire the consolations of belonging and so often make their choices for the wrong reasons.

Once committed, guard against running away. When Buddhism really begins to 'work', things often get difficult – sometimes very difficult. One may, for instance, have to face things in oneself that one has been dodging for years. The ego does not open itself to new growth without a struggle either – and sometimes an intense one, for every advance demands a kind of death to one's old self. And there are phases when things seem to go dead, like walking through endless, monotonous mud and sleet; or when agonising doubts or fears arise. Remember the night that the Buddha spent beneath the Bodhi Tree before his Enlightenment. Mara has his ways of trying to deflect us. Try therefore to follow the Buddha's example and not be deterred.

On the other hand, do not feel afraid to leave a group or teacher when it is clear that they have ceased to work for you. Again there can be gross or subtle pressure against going: it may be stigmatised as defection, disloyalty or failure. But remember, Shakyamuni Buddha himself was not afraid to leave his teachers when he had absorbed all they had to teach him. Nor was he deterred from discarding practices he had decided were not useful from fear that fellow practitioners would spurn or deride him. Always, however, be watchful: delve into your own motivations, check your responses and feelings, and keep a clear eye on what is happening around you, avoiding the extremes of being a destructive critic or a starry-eyed naïve. The Buddhist Way is the middle way – and it is all about learning. If you do decide to leave a group or teacher, do so if possible in the proper way, with appropriate gratitude.

Always be realistic and do not fall prey to illusions, especially collective ones. One illusion that besets many newcomers is that religion is good per se, so they expect all the people and institutions they encounter to be thoroughly benign. In fact, with rare exceptions, religious people and institutions are much like worldly ones. They have their dark as well as their light sides. So be watchful on this account, and then perhaps you will not be too disillusioned if, for instance, your teacher, though possessing undeniable virtues and talents, also turns out to have feet of clay.

Also do not be bedazzled by charismatic teachers, or ones with mass followings, or great fame, power or worldly wealth. True teachers have perennially kept a low profile, living in seclusion, not seeking crowds or worldly success. What they taught was difficult, for the few rather than for the many. Those who successfully mass-market spiritual teachings often do so by watering them down and adding seductive sweeteners.

Be careful too of teachers and groups that pressure you for money or services. The Dharma is said to be beyond price, something that should be freely given. A monk does not ask for dana; he waits for it silently. It should be left up to you to contribute as and when and to what extent you feel fit. Try for your part to be generous, however, not least because generosity fosters spiritual growth.

We go to teachers and groups at the beginning because we need information, guidance and the support of like-minded people. But always the main aim in Buddhism is to help the individual to become free, autonomous, self-reliant. The teacher or group that helps you achieve this is therefore healthy and right-directed. Sadly today, however, there exist many cults that do not liberate their devotees but in effect stunt their devolopment and deprive them of their autonomy. This happens because it is possible for a guru to go astray, and also because the devotee can collude in his or her own exploitation and enslavement. As it is hard to grow up and become an adult, there is always the temptation to look for the ultimate good parent, someone who will make one's decisons and mould one's life. This is to become a sheep or a bond-slave, but it is comfortable to be a sheep or a bond-slave. One does not have to think or act for oneself!

Always, therefore, maintain a centre of strength and self-reliance within yourself. Do not be pressured out of it. Remember that, as an adult, whatever you think, say or do is your own responsibility. It cannot be handed over to another. And resist the temptation to get too close to a teacher so as to enjoy his or her approval, or to become special, like a favoured son or daughter. Do not stand too far off either. There is a Tibetan saying that the guru is like a fire. Stand too close and you will get burned; stand too far away and you will not get the benefit of any heat – in fact you will freeze!

A word about the ego. There is nowadays a lot of ego-bashing in spiritual circles, the old 'I' being relentlessly blamed for all our own and the world's woes. In fact the ego is only problematic if its development has been stultified or if there is exclusive clinging to it. A healthy, stable ego, on the other hand, is an absolute necessity for successful functioning in the world. Without one higher spiritual development cannot be safely undertaken and one can get stuck in all kinds of negative states, perhaps suffering much psychological pain – and certainly never fulfilling one's potential. Part of one's work may therefore be to heal old wounds and generally bring one's ego up to par. In this context many seekers have found the modern Western psychotherapies very useful. Once that is realised, however, trans-egoic development may begin – that is, opening to that which is beyond 'me'.

It is a moot point whether truly 'selfless persons' who have no ego can exist. We can certainly wean ourself away from exclusive identification with the ego and open to the trans-egoic, but I wonder whether the ego can ever fully die out while the psycho-physical organism walks the earth – or indeed if it is desirable that it should. Perhaps, then, ego and trans-ego exist together in the realised person, in a kind of harmony or balance – but now I am beginning to speculate . . .

If the spiritual quest is a great adventure, it must have its difficulties and dangers Nothing worthwhile is ever achieved by staying at home in safety and comfort. One has to throw oneself into the unknown and brave its mysteries. There are many pit-falls on the path, some of which we have touched upon above, but the greatest of all is spiritual inflation. This is a dire condition in which the ego is enlarged, blown up like a balloon. In traditional terms, it means that we are not dealing with a human being but one engulfed or possessed by primordial energies – a demonaic being in fact. This can happen because tremendous psycho-spiritual energies are generated by practice, especially in Tantra. These energies are not simply good in themselves; they are neutral and can be turned to any number of purposes. They can certainly be used to allow us to grow beyond ourselves, to transcend the ego; but the ego can also appropriate them and use them for its own selfish ends. Gurus and teachers are particularly vulnerable to this, for they enjoy power, prestige and public acclaim and so are very susceptible to corruption. It is difficult not to have your head turned when dozens of people stare at you in wide-eyed awe every day. You easily begin to think you are special – unless you maintain close awareness and keep the tendency in check. Inflation makes authentic spiritual development impossible, because an inflated ego is so much more difficult to let go of than an ordinary one.

How to detect inflation? Watch out for the presence of the power complex: the desire to rule and control. This often goes with a certain ruthlessness and contempt for the well-being of others, as though they are of no account and so can be used and abused at will, whereas the guru is great and nothing should be allowed to stand in the way of his or her manifest destiny. An intense dislike of being disagreed with, questioned or criticised are other symptoms; also an eagerness to spend time with and recruit the rich and famous. A liking for titles and fine robes, too, hearing the sound of one's own voice proclaiming inspired truth, and little personal indulgences and concessions, including sometimes a laxness in practice, as though, having 'got there', it is no longer necessary to keep up basic disciplines.

Every practitioner, even the beginner, should be vigilant at all times. This is the basic safeguard, and must be kept up particularly at times when things seem to be going well and one thinks one is 'making progress'. In any case, never regard 'spiritual achievements' as personal gains.

There is another pit-fall, and one into which I personally have fallen. I call it being a prestige Buddhist. I mean by this becoming a functionary of a Buddhist group: an administrator, editor, committee person, teacher or office-holder of any kind. On the face of it, such things look very much like right livelihood. One is, after all, serving the Dharma – and if one can do it professionally, so much the better. What happens, however, is that one somehow gets diverted from one's basic practice as the other work takes over. And it can have inflating effects too: a person sitting on a religious committee can enjoy a high profile and a spiritual status quite uncommensurate with his or her actual spiritual attainment. It is perhaps no coincidence, therefore, that life in Buddhist centres can, for those running them, become quite fraught.

Also do not use Buddhism as an escape from the world or the problems of social living. It is easy to get hooked on a kind of 'Ivory Tower Buddhism', where the rest of the world can go hang while you concentrate on the great task of your own spiritual salvation. The Buddha himself, when occasion demanded, was never reluctant to intervene in social situations; and he even made political pronouncements. On the other hand, one is never so vulnerable to being bushwhacked by the ego as when one is caught up in righteous indignation over a worthy cause. We easily forget then that darkness exists in us too, not just in the evil men whom we oppose. Do we really want to help the world's victims – or bask in the indulgent pleasure of being 'one of the goodies'?

Do not expect too much of yourself at the beginning. Real and lasting change is a long, slow business. Practise regularly and conscientiously, but do not become some kind of spiritual athlete trying to break records. You do not have to sit in meditation longer than anyone else, bear more pain in your knees, read more books. In fact, that driven, competitive energy will probably wear you out pretty quickly.

In the same way, do not turn your practice into a kind of penance, flagellating yourself with it. We Westerners do not really think very well of ourselves; we suffer from deep-seated guilts and self-hatred. Because of this, we are hard on ourselves – and hard on others too. Look what brutality has been inflicted on the world in the name of righteous religion. What we really need, therefore, is to soften up, to open our hardened hearts and allow our innate but stifled warmth to emerge. This is indeed what Buddhist practice is very much about, especially the Mahayana variety with its primary emphasis on compassion.

There are forms of Buddhist practice, however, that are very hard and harsh. While those may have been appropriate in the areas and situations in which they were originally developed, it is doubtful whether they are always beneficial for hard-nosed Westerners, who often need more of the opposite treatment. Some people are drawn to those hard forms, though. Perhaps they feel that, through them, they can place themselves beyond suffering. But you do not conquer suffering by becoming like a block of ice or a rigid, programmed automaton. In Buddhism, we train ourselves to be open and fully vulnerable to the sting of suffering – but able to take it and survive. We train ourselves to be real human beings.

While being aware of the pit-falls of the path, do not be deterred by them. You will certainly make mistakes. We all make mistakes – and they are all right, if we learn from them. You may have your ideals smashed; people in whom you invest great trust may let you down; but do not cling to the negativity such experiences inevitably produce. Let go of it, absorb the lesson – and walk on.

Always try to remain open. You cannot learn if you are not open – and open-minded. You never know from which unlikely direction your next important teaching is going to come. Unfortunately, though, probably because they have been hurt or disillusioned early on, many Westerners close up and so cannot take in anything that might change or even help them. Open-ness means being fully alert and aware, not blocking anything out, not avoiding things (especially unpleasant things), not saying No, not refusing to meet the world on anything but one's own terms. It means letting go of the need to control. However, be realistic too; do not continue to be open when it is clear it is no longer sensible to be so. Openness is not synonymous with naïveté or gullibility. The middle way again . . .

When your knowledge begins to deepen and insights come, do not become rigid in your views. Having wandered lost in the wilderness for many years, it is very tempting, when things begin to clarify, to formulate a new, improved world-view and then, smug in one's achievement, cling tenaciously to it – and even become enthused with missionary zeal. Time and again I have blithely thought that I had everything worked out, the meaning of life in the palm of my hand . . . only to have egg spattered on my face as my beautiful world-picture crumbled under life's batterings. All ideas in the mind, however lofty or insightful, are temporary and imperfect. The goal of Buddhist practice is to let them all go.

It is all, however, as I said at the start, a great adventure – and especially for beginners, who are often so much more fresh and open than long-term seekers. The Zen master Shunryu Suzuki Roshi, who worked for many years in the USA, had good reason to call his most famous book *Zen Mind, Beginner's Mind*. I remember with great nostalgia the early days of my own quest, as I ranged for many months through India as the spirit moved me. I had expected to meet great gurus, but the swamis and sadhus who confidently proclaimed their saintly accomplishments in the various ashrams and holy places I visited failed to impress me. I was not let down, though; I received my teaching from India herself, that deeply spiritual land where, whether one goes with it or resists, one is precipitated into stark confrontation with this amazing business of life in which we find ourselves so mysteriously caught up. Wonderful experiences and insights came, not earned but free gifts bestowed by the Unknowable with bountiful generosity.

This is in many ways a good time to explore Buddhism. Any spiritual tradition has a lot of the true spirit in it when it is new or undergoing a new phase of development. Before too long the infrastructure of an organised 'church' will no doubt emerge (in fact we are beginning to see the beginnings of this) and, as we know from past experience, churches, with their worldly endowments and armies of paid professionals, nearly always suppress that anarchic spiritual tradition that places primary emphasis on direct mystical insight – on seeing the truth for oneself. If one so wishes, one can certainly go to Buddhism for the conventional consolations of religion, but one exchanges one's birthright for a mess of pottage by doing so. The function of authentic spirituality is not to provide security and solace but to encourage the seeker to venture out on the lonely and difficult path of self-knowledge.

So do not be intimidated. Have confidence in your own spiritual potentiality, your ability to find your own unique way. Learn from others certainly, and use what you find useful, but also learn to trust your own inner wisdom. Have courage. Be awake and aware. Remember too that Buddhism is not about being 'a Buddhist'; that is, obtaining a new identity tag. Nor is it about collecting head-knowledge, practices and techniques. It is ultimately about letting go of all forms and concepts and becoming free.

So be prepared to cut through all superfluous accretions and go for the gold of the spiritual core. It is certainly there, within – and, so the greatest masters assure us, it is not as difficult to get at as we often tend to think.

NOTES AND REFERENCES

INTRODUCTION

1. The question is often asked by modern Western Buddhists whether these realms, especially the hell realms, are 'real' or metaphors for psychological states. In the Buddhist scriptures they are certainly depicted as real and the faithful of traditional Buddhist countries certainly regard them as such. However, this does not settle the matter. Religious teachers and writers have often resorted to creating lurid hell realms for pragmatic reasons, in order to discourage their followers from 'evil'.

CHAPTER 2

1. It is also called by other names: for example, the Mantrayana or Secret Mantra school, though this probably originated at an early phase.

2. *The Buddhism of Tibet and the Key to the Middle Way*, Tenzin Gyatso, the Fourteenth Dalai Lama, London, 1975, p. 30.

3. 'Buddhism in India' by L. Gomez, in *The Encyclopaedia of Religion*, vol. 2, ed, M, Éliade, New York and London, 1987, p. 377.

CHAPTER 4

1. *Four Quartets*, T.S. Eliot ('Dry Salvages' section), paperback edition, London, 1956, p. 39.

2. *The Colossus of Maroussi*, Henry Miller, paperback edition, London, 1950, p. 203.

3. *Dhammapada*, chapter 1, verse 1.

4. Actually we should not talk of a single consciousness traversing the bardo.

It is more like a stream of causally-interconnected consciousness moments. We could therefore call it a 'consciousness continuum'.

5. *Walden*, by H.D. Thoreau, reprinted in *Thoreau: Walden & Other Writings*, ed. J.W. Krutch, New York, 1962, p. 108.

6. Adapted from *The Tiger's Cave*, Trevor Leggett, paperback edition, London, 1977, p. 160.

7. From 'Under Ben Bulben', in *The Collected Poems of W.B. Yeats*, London, 1961, p. 401.

8. *Majjhima Nikaya*, 245–6.

CHAPTER 5

1. *Majjhima Nikaya*, 36.

2. *Majjhima Nikaya*, 49; and, in slightly different form, in *Digha Nikaya* 11.

3. Actually, the notion of Shunyata arose among the Hinayana schools, but it was fully developed in and became one of the benchmarks of the Mahayana.

4. The following is based upon Stephen Batchelor's translation of Shantideva's *Bodhisattvacharyavatara*, reprinted, Library of Tibetan Works & Archives, Dharamsala, 1987.

5. *The Short Prajñaparamita Texts*, trans. E. Conze, London, 1973, p. 138.

6. The negativistic hard-line was meanwhile perpetuated by the Prasangika sub-school of Buddhapalita and his colleagues.

7. *Seven Works of Vasubandhu*, trans. Stephan Anacker, Varanasi, 1984, p. 189.

8. *The Flower Adornment Sutra*, vol. 3 trans. Thoman Cleary, Boston, 1987, pp. 365–6.

CHAPTER 6

1. *The Lankavatara Sutra*, trans. D.T. Suzuki, London, 1932, p. 219.

2. *Idle Jottings*, Zen Reflections from the Tsure-zure Gusa of Yoshida Kenko, ed. Irwin Switzer III, Totnes, 1988, p. 36.

3. *The Life of the Buddha*, Ven. Nyanamoli, Kandy, 1978, p. 158.

4. *A Guide to the Bodhisattva's Way of Life*, Shantideva, trans. S. Batchelor, Dharamsala, 1979, p. 106.

CHAPTER 7

1. 'Satipatthana Sutta' from Vol. 1 of the *Majjhima Nikaya*, trans. I.B. Horner, Reprinted Leicester, 1988, pp 5–6.

2. *Buddhist Dictionary*, Ven. Nyanatiloka, revised and enlarged edition, Kandy, 1972, p. 44.

3. *'Madhyantavibhagabhasya'*, Vasubandhu, Chapter 4, trans. Stefan Anacker in *Mahayana Buddhist Meditation*, ed. M. Kiyota, Honolulu, 1978, pp. 106-7, p.91.

4. 'The Song of Meditation', Hakuin Zenji, trans. Trevor Leggett in *A First Zen Reader*, Rutland & Tokyo, 1960, p. 67

5. 'Rules for Zazen' (Zazen-gi), trans. D. Welch and K. Tanahashi, in *Moon in a Dewdrop: Writings of Zen Master Dogen*, ed. K. Tanahashi, UK edition Shaftesbury 1988, p. 30.

6. Ibid., p. 152.

7. *Zen Master Hakuin: Selected Writings*, trans. P. B. Yampolsky, New York, 1971, pp. 118ff.

8. *The Rain of Wisdom*, trans. Nalanda Translation Committee, Boulder, 1980, p. 90.

9. *The Crystal & the Way of Light: The Teachings of Namkhai Norbu*, ed. John Shane, London, 1986, p. 12.

CHAPTER 8

1. The suffix -*pa* denotes a person. Thus a Nyingmapa is a person who adheres to the Nyingma school. The Western plural form -*pas*, now in popular use, denotes a quantity of people, or in this case the followers of the school.

2. Introduction to *The History of the Sakya Tradition*, by Chogay Trichen, Bristol, 1983, p. x.

3. *The Jewelled Staircase*, by Geshe Wangyal, Ithaca, N.Y., 1986, p. 62.

4. 'Love, Altruism, Vegetarianism, Anger & the Responsibilities of Teachers', H.H. the Dalai Lama, in *The Middle Way*, Vol. 60, No. 2, p. 68.

5. *The Sayings & Doings of Pai-chang*, trans. Thomas Cleary, Los Angeles, 1978, pp. 18–19.

6. *The Zen Teaching of Huang-po*, trans. J. Blofeld, reprint, London, 1971, p. 63.

7. *The Zen Teaching of Hui-hai on Instantaneous Enlightenment*, trans. John Blofeld, reprint, Leicester, 1987, p. 49. Blofeld's Hui-hai is the same person as Cleary's Pai-chang.

8. Loc. cit., p. 75.

9. *Bankei Zen*, by Peter Haskel, New York, 1984, p. 13.

10. *The Zen Master Hakuin: Selected Writings*, trans. P.B. Yampolsky, New York, 1971, pp. 144–5.

11. *Shinran's Gospel of Pure Faith*, Alfred Bloom, Tucson, Arizona, 1965 (reprint 1981), p. 1.

FURTHER
READING

TEXTS

THERAVADA TEXTS

The Pali Text Society (73 Lime Walk, Headington, Oxford OX3 7AD, UK) has concerned itself with making the Pali Canon available in English translation. Its publications include volumes of suttas of the *Digha Nikaya* (Long Discourses), *Majjhima Nikaya* (Middle Length Discourses) and *Samyutta Nikaya* (the 'Kindred Sayings'). They also publish T.W. Rhys-Davids' and W. Stede's *Pali-English Dictionary* and a useful *Introduction to Pali* by A.K. Warder (1984). Wisdom Publications have meanwhile brought out a new translation of the *Digha Nikaya* by M. O'C. Walshe, entitled *Thus Have I Heard* (London, 1987).

MAHAYANA TEXTS

A Guide to the Bodhisattva's Way of Life. Shantideva, trans. S. Batchelor, Library of Tibetan Works & Archives, Dharamsala, 1979.
The Short Prajñaparamita Texts, trans. E. Conze, Luzac, London, 1973.
Buddhist Wisdom Books, trans. E. Conze, George Allen & Unwin, London, 1958, (the Diamond and Heart sutras).
The Awakening of Faith in the Mahayana, Ashvaghosa, trans.

Y.S. Hakeda, Columbia University Press, New York, 1967.

The Holy Teaching of Vimalakirti, trans. R.H.F. Thurman, Pennsylvania State University Press, University Park, 1986.

The Lankavatara Sutra, trans. D.T. Suzuki, Routledge, London, 1932.

Seven Works of Vasubandhu, trans. S. Anaker, Motilal Banarsidass, Delhi, 1984.

The Threefold Lotus Sutra, trans. Kato, Tamura et al. Kosei Publishing Co., Tokyo, 1987.

The Avatamsaka Sutra, (3 vols.) trans. T. Cleary, Shambhala, Boston, 1985–7.

ZEN TEXTS

The Zen Teaching of Huang-po, trans. J. Blofeld, The Buddhist Society, London, 1968.

The Record of Rinzai, trans. I Schloegl, The Buddhist Society, London, 1975.

The Platform Sutra of the 6th Patriarch (Hui Neng), trans. P. Yampolsky, Columbia University Press, New York, 1967.

Zen Master Hakuin: Selected Writings, trans. P. Yampolsky, Columbia University Press, New York, 1971.

The Blue Cliff Record (3 vols.) trans. T. & J.C. Cleary, Shambhala, Boulder 1977.

Swampland Flowers: The Letters & Lectures of Zen Master Ta Hui, trans. C. Cleary, Grove Press, New York, 1977.

Bankei Zen, trans. P. Haskel, Grove Press, New York, 1984.

The Zen Teaching of Instantaneous Awakening, Hui Hai, trans. J. Blofeld, reprint, Buddhist Publishing Group, Leicester, 1987.

Shobogenzo: Zen Essays by Dogen Zenji, trans. T. Cleary, University of Hawaii Press, Honolulu, 1986.

Two Zen Classics: Mumonkan & Hekiganroku, trans. K. Sekida, Weatherhill, New York & Tokyo, 1977.

TANTRIC TEXTS

The Kalachakra Tantra: Rite of Initiation, trans. J. Hopkins, Wisdom Publications, London, 1985.

Tantra in Tibet: The Great Exposition of Secret Mantra, Tsongkhapa, George Allen & Unwin, London, 1976.

STUDIES

GENERAL

The World of Buddhism, ed. Béchert and Gombrich, Thames & Hudson, London, 1985.
The Buddhist Handbook, John Snelling, Century-Hutchinson, London, 1987.

REFERENCE

A Popular Dictionary of Buddhism, Christmas Humphreys, Arco, London, 1962.
Buddhist Dictionary, Nyanatiloka Thera, Buddhist Publication Society, Kandy, 1980.
The Buddhist Directory, The Buddhist Society, London, 1987.
Zen Buddhism in North America, A History & Directory, Zen Lotus Society, Toronto, 1986.

THE BUDDHIST WORLD-VIEW

Buddhist Cosmology, R. Kloetzli, Motilal Banarsidass, Delhi, 1983.

THE BUDDHA

The Life of the Buddha, Bhikkhu Ñyanamoli, Buddhist Publication Society, Kandy, 1971.
The Buddha, Trevor Ling, Penguin Books, Harmondsworth, 1973.

MEDITATION

Living Buddhist Masters, Jack Kornfield, reprint, Shambhala Publications, Boulder, 1983.
The Heart of Buddhist Meditation, Nyanaponika Thera, Rider Books, London, 1962.
Mahayana Buddhist Meditation: Theory & Practice, ed. Minoru Kiyota, University of Hawaii Press, Honolulu, 1978.

INDIAN BUDDHISM

History of Indian Buddhism, É. Lamotte, trans. S. Webb-Boin. Peeters Press, Louvain, 1988.
Indian Buddhism, K. Warder, Motilal Banarsidass, Delhi, 1970, reprint 1980.

THERAVADA BUDDHISM

What the Buddha Taught, W. Rahula, Gordon Frazer, Bedford, 1972.
Cittaviveka, Ajahn Sumedho, Chithurst Forest Monastery, Petersfield, 1983.
Theravada Buddhism, R. Gombrich, Routledge & Kegan Paul, London, 1988.

MAHAYANA BUDDHISM (GENERAL)

Mahayana Buddhism, Paul Williams, Kegan Paul, London, 1989.

VAJRAYANA/TANTRA

see TIBETAN BUDDHISM below

BUDDHIST PHILOSOPHY

Essentials of Buddhist Philosophy, J. Takakusu, reprint Motilal Banarsidass, Delhi, 1975.
The Central Conception of Buddhism (and the Meaning of the World 'Dharma'), T. Stcherbatsky, London 1923, reprint Motilal Banarsidass, Delhi, 1970.
The Central Philosophy of Buddhism, T.R.V. Murti, George Allen & Unwin, London, 1955. (A study of the Madhyamaka system.)
Entry into the Inconceivable: An Introduction to Hua-yen Buddhism, Thomas Cleary, University of Hawaii Press, Honolulu, 1983.
Hua-yen Buddhism: The Jewel Net of Indra, Francis Cook, Pennsylvania State University Press, University Park, 1981.
Studies in the Lankavatara Sutra, D.T. Suzuki, Routledge, London, 1930.

CHINESE BUDDHISM

Buddhism in Chinese History, A.F. Wright, Stamford University Press, Stamford, 1965.
Buddhism in China, K. Chen, Princeton University Press, Princeton, 1964.

PURE LAND

Shinran's Gospel of Pure Grace, Alfred Bloom, University of Arizona Press, Tucson, Arizona, 1965, reprint 1981.
Plain Words on the Pure Land Way, trans. D. Hirota, Ryukoku University, Kyoto, 1989.

NICHIREN

Nichiren Shoshu Buddhism, R. Causton, Century, London, 1988.

CHINESE & JAPANESE ZEN

A History of Zen Buddhism, H. Dumoulin, Faber, London, 1968.
A First Zen Reader, T. Leggett, Charles Tuttle, Tokyo & Rutland, Vermont, 1960.
Zen & the Ways, T. Leggett, RKP, London, 1978.
Taking the Path of Zen, Robert Aitken, North Point Press, San Francisco, 1982.
Unsui: A Diary of a Zen Monk, Giei Sato & Eshin Nishimura, University of Hawaii Press, Honolulu, 1973.
Empty Cloud: The Autobiography of Chinese Zen Master Xu Yun, trans. C. Luk, Element Books, Dorset, 1988.

KOREAN ZEN

The Way of Korean Zen, Kusan Sunim, trans. M. Fages, Weatherhill, New York & Tokyo, 1985.

TIBETAN BUDDHISM

The Jewel in the Lotus, ed. S. Batchelor, Wisdom Publications, London, 1987.

Advice from a Spiritual Friend, Geshe Rabten & Geshe Dhargyey, Wisdom Publications, London, 1978.
The Religions of Tibet, G. Tucci, RKP, London, 1980.
Hidden Teachings of Tibet, Tulku Thondup Rinpoche, Wisdom Publications, London, 1986.
The Crystal & the Way of Light, Namkhai Norbu Rinpoche, RKP, London, 1986.

WESTERN BUDDHISM

Buddhism in Britain, P. Oliver, Rider Books, London, 1979.
How the Swans Came to the Lake, R. Fields, revised edition, Shambhala, Boston, 1986 (Buddhism in the USA).

BUDDHISM & WESTERN PSYCHOLOGY

Psychotherapy East & West, Alan Watts, Ballantine Books, New York, 1961.
Buddhism & Western Psychology, Nathan Katz, Shambhala, Boulder, 1983.
Psychology & the East, C.G. Jung, RKP, London, 1978.

BUDDHISM & SOCIAL ACTION

The Social Face of Buddhism (An Approach to Social & Political Activism), Ken Jones, Wisdom Publications, London, 1989.
Being Peace, Thich Nhat Hanh, Parallax Press, Berkeley, 1987.

WOMEN & BUDDHISM

Women of Wisdom. Tsultrim Allione, RKP, London, 1984.
Meetings with Remarkable Women: Buddhist Teachers in America, L. Friedman, Shambhala, Boston, 1987.

JOURNALS & BOOK SERVICE

BUDDHIST JOURNALS

Buddhism Now, published by BPG, Sharpham North, Ashprington, Totnes, S. Devon, TQ9 7UT, UK.

Buddhist Studies Review, 31 Russell Chambers, Bury Place, London WC1A 2JX.

Inquiring Mind, published by Insight Meditation Society, PO Box 9999, North Berkeley Station, Berkeley, CA 94709, USA.

The Middle Way, published by The Buddhist Society, 58 Eccleston Sq., London SW1V 1PH, UK.

Sangha Newletter, published by English Sangha Trust, Amaravati, Gt. Gaddesden, Hemel Hempstead, Herts HP1 3BZ, UK.

Vajradhatu Sun, published by Vajradhatu (Chögyam Trungpa organization), 1345 Spruce St., Boulder, CO 80302, USA.

BUDDHIST BOOK SERVICE

Wisdom Publications:

Britain: 402 Hoe St., London E17 9AA. (tel. 081–520 5588)

USA: 361 Newbury St., Boston, MA 02115. (tel. (617) 536–3358)

Australia: PO Box 1326, Chatswood, NSW 2067. (tel. (02) 922–6338)

INDEX